God Is Great

TONIA JENKINS

hatherleigh

Hatherleigh Press is committed to preserving and protecting the natural
resources of the Earth. Environmentally responsible and sustainable
practices are embraced within the company's mission statement.

Hatherleigh Press is a member of the Publishers Earth Alliance, committed to preserving and protecting the natural resources of the planet while
developing a sustainable business model for the book publishing industry.

Library of Congress Cataloging-in-Publication Data is available.

ISBN 978-1-57826-292-2

All Hatherleigh Press titles are available for bulk purchase, special promo-
tions, and premiums. For information on reselling and special purchase
opportunities, call 1-800-733-3000 and ask for the Special Sales Manager.

Interior design by DC Designs
Cover design by Nick Macagnone

www.hatherleighpress.com

10 9 8 7 6 5 4 3 2 1
Printed in the United States

DEDICATION

THIS BOOK IS DEDICATED to you, Lord. Without your power, love, and grace I could not have done this. You are an amazing and awesome God.

When I think of the many times you have spared my life, I scream on the inside of your greatness. You have taught me to love and to be compassionate towards your people. You have instilled in me a desire to help and have concern for your people. I have learned how to be patient yet diligent in seeking your direction. In spite of my own selfish ways, you have patiently loved me. Regardless of how I stopped or was disobedient, it was your love that covered me. It is you, Lord, that has made me the woman I am today. It is my endeavor to continually persevere in all that you have for me to do. For I realize that the work that I do is to glorify your name. I have to let my light shine. So, because of you, here is a tool to witness your infinite love towards man. You have taught me to have a heart of servitude. Your love extends and goes beyond any man's imagination. The thought of you giving me the privilege to write this book amazes me. I am humbled and honored in you, Lord. My experiences with you, Lord, grow deeper and greater than I ever imagined. I continually submit my will unto you that you would have your way in my life. To think that all you ask of us is to respond to your presence with worship and praise is awesome. Your guidance is a compass to life's pathways. As I continue to develop in every spiritual aspect of you, God, my craving and understanding intensifies, stimulates growth in grace, fortifies against doubt and encourages personal witnessing and strengthens me and others for a healthy Christian life and service. God, you are so Great!

—Pastor Tonia Jenkins

This book is also dedicated to two of the greatest men I have ever known:

FIRST, TO MY DAD, THE LATE
JOHN CURTIS GRADY:

You will always be remembered in my heart.

I love you more than words could ever express. You taught me how to push past whatever was in my way. I'll always remember the calls you would make ("Hey, stinker, are you alright?"). Your voice would brighten my day; sometimes a tear would fall. I love you, Dad. I will never forget you.

I remember running home to you with a diploma in my hand, saying, "I did it, Dad!" Well, I did it again!

Until we meet again,
Love you,
Your daughter, "Baby Girl" Tonia

TO MY FATHER-IN-LAW, THE BELOVED BISHOP
DR. RAYMOND A. JENKINS:

You were another father to me. You will always be remembered in my heart.

You taught me spiritually and I will never forget you. Your famous words, "Oh, come on now," let me know it wasn't that bad. You told me to praise my way through and here I am, praising my way through.

I love you, "Pop."

Acknowledgements

To DARREN JENKINS: Thank you for being a dedicated husband. You always taught me to be committed to whatever I set out to do. Thank you for your support and faithfulness. Your richness in the word of God has made me rich in spirit. Your meticulous help has made this book come alive. I could not have done this without you.

To NICOLE, DARREN JR., AND BRIANNA: I thank God for your very existence. You were my cheerleading team. You helped me and gave me reason for going on. You bring me so much joy. My children, you are the best.

To MY MOTHER MARY: Wow, to be adorned with such a great name. So fitting. Your perseverance in life has placed you in position to be named after one of the greatest women on earth. You have been an inspiration to me throughout my life. You are an amazing woman. Strong, full of wisdom, and powerful. Thank you for your prayers and support. I love you, Mom.

To DANETTE (NET), CHARLES, AND CHRIS: My sister and brothers, thank you for your support. You have always been there when I needed you most.

To LARRY AND CHARLENE RIVERS: My friends, you have been so dedicated from the beginning. Your life has helped me see and understand what true friendship is. I don't see you often enough, but I feel your prayers. Thank you for being you.

To SHARINATL INGRAM, MY SISTER AND FRIEND IN CHRIST: Thank you for being a faithful friend and prayer partner. You have been strength and inspiration to me far more than I could ever tell you.

To MY CHURCH FAMILY, NEW HOPE LOVE CENTER MINISTRIES: Thank you for your love, patience, kindness, graciousness, and untiring work efforts. You helped make this happen.

To MOTHER FEREEBE AND MOTHER HULEN: Thank you for your love, your prayers.

To ORA JENKINS, MY MOTHER-IN-LAW AND MY FIRST PASTOR MOM: Thank you for your wealth and knowledge in God. I will never forget the labor of love you poured into me. You have given me more encouragement than you could imagine.

To HATHERLEIGH, MY CO-WORKERS AND TO THE EDITORS: Thank you for believing in me. Thank you for your encouragement. You are truly a great group of people and I love you all.

To ANDREW FLACH: Without you this could not have happened. Because you had a yielded heart you gave me this opportunity. I really thank God for you. You have really been an inspiring instrument in my life. You have encouraged me to reach for the best and nothing less. Your faithfulness and your open heart will bring you great prosperity in God. Love you always.

To all my family and friends in the body of Christ whose names are too long to list: I want you to know that I love you all and your thoughts and prayers were appreciated. You will never be forgotten. Thank you for your support and inspiration. Let us all continue to work diligently in the body of Christ.

Wenda Castro: Thank you for trusting me for the job you did so well. You are a great friend.

About the Stories in This Book

This book features true stories from real people. Many of these stories are from women I have known through a group called Women of Substance.

When I think of these women and how they scaled amazing heights despite obstacles in their way, I feel so inspired. Their stories remind me of the greatness God has placed in all of us. Watching so many of these women has sparked an energy in me that surges every time I think of them. I'm reminded of how our energy actually needs to run: there has to be a negative to meet with the positive in order for the current to flow.

As hard as the negative tried to overtake the positive in these women's lives, their perseverance made them triumphant. Through them, I'm inspired to encourage and push our young women into greater lives. For every story told gives someone new hope that their life does not end with what they have encountered. Instead, it begins with the encounter and ends with a victorious life. The victory is with God: each one held on to God, reached back and worked with what they had to push forward. Each woman has received their recovery, revived, restored, refreshed and redeemed.

Each one of us has a story to tell. Your story is what you make it to be. Take courage when you hear the tales of the lives of others. Your story may have similarities or may be different entirely. Make it your own.

Contents

VICTORIOUS *by Pastor Darren Jenkins* **41**

I COME CLOSER *by Pastor Darren Jenkins* **117**

Foreword

Each one of us was created in the image of God. I was inspired to write this book to help form a deeper understanding of the magnificent ways God plays a role in all our lives. Each of the 52 chapters, one for each Sunday of the year, presents insight into how awesome and miraculous our God is.

The Bible selections, quotes, and personal stories, have all been carefully chosen as representations of the supreme bond that we each have with God. Many of these chapters feature stories that are true life experiences. These may remind you of something that you or someone you know has endured at one time or another. I sincerely hope these stories of triumph inspire you to keep going.

No matter what difficulties you are facing, you can use the insights in this book to help you strengthen your relationship with God.

As you experience challenging times, as well as moments of joy, may this book remind you of God's awesome power and His presence in our lives.

MERCY

Let Your power fill this place
Oh mercy, mercy, mercy

You are the song that fills my soul
With just one touch, You made me whole
It was Your mercy that saw beyond who I am

—from the song written and composed by
  Pastor Darren Jenkins

‖‖

"Frequently remind yourself that God is with you, that He will never fail you, that you can count upon him. Say these words, 'God is with me, helping me.'"

—Norman Vincent Peale

‖‖

1

God IS Your Guide

You may be faced with struggles and circumstances today that seem insurmountable. It may seem like there is no possible answer or way out. I ask you to try and trust the great God I serve.

OFTEN, WE GO THROUGH LIFE not understanding our purpose and the plan that God has for us.

When I look back on all of the challenges and circumstances that seemed at the time to overtake me, I realize that each trial was a building block to strengthen me. When people look at me today, they cannot believe that I went through what I did.

One of the hardest phases in my life occurred when I left my home at the tender age of 14. At the time, something on the inside of me was screaming to get out. My mother and father tried everything within their power to find help for me, but I just cried, unable to express what I was feeling. My parents both worked and provided a good life for our family. I had a great home, food on the table, and a bed on which to lay my head. Yet there was a pull within me. So I left home.

Then I was on my own. I slept outside many cold dark nights, spent time in places where no young lady should go. Deep down inside, I knew something was wrong. I knew that I could return home, but pride had overtaken me. When you are young and feel that you are always right, then it seems everyone else is always wrong. Looking back I wonder: What could I possibly have known at the age of 14?

I found myself alone with nowhere to turn, left to make the best of the choices I had made. I had to make adult decisions with a child's mind.

Eventually, I settled down with a family who attended church. I did not understand everything at first. But then, one day—within what seemed like mere moments—I was pulled toward an overwhelming feeling of love. I had always known that my parents and my family loved me, but this was a love I had never experienced before. Even more remarkable, I could not see this God that was being proclaimed—but I knew that His love was real. I wanted to experience more of this love, and I wanted to share it with everyone.

The Bible tells us that God gives each one of us "a measure of faith." As I searched for understanding about what I was experiencing, I followed my faith. I learned that my faith in God was increased by my belief in Him. I realized that I *must* have had faith in God all along to go out on my own at the age of 14 and think that I could make it.

At the age of 15, I wholeheartedly received God into my life.

As I grew, I continued to face difficult challenges. However, I continued to pray and trust that God would lead and guide me in life through any maze. I eventually went back home to my family. I was not as happy about returning to them as I wanted to be, for I was pregnant. But I needed my family, and they received me with open arms.

My parents had always instilled in me the importance of an education, and I had always wanted to finish school and get a diploma. So, despite my circumstances, I continued to go to school. Even though I knew I would run into people who knew about my situation, I was determined. I pressed forward and eventually achieved my goal: I received my diploma. I was married at the age of 18, and I am still married today. My husband and I have three children: one of my daughters is currently attending college, and my son is preparing to attend college in January of 2010. My youngest daughter will graduate from high school in 2010.

My experiences in life may be familiar to many. You may be faced with struggles and circumstances today that seem insurmountable. It may seem like there is no possible answer or way out.

I ask you to try and trust the great God I serve.

God is great.

Now faith is the assurance of things hoped for, the conviction of things not seen.

Hebrews 11:1

|||||||||||||||||||||||||||||||||||||||||||||||||||||||||||||||||||||||||||||||||||||||

"We were born to make manifest the glory of God within us."

—Marianne Williamson,
*A Return To Love: Reflections on the
Principles of A Course in Miracles*

|||||||||||||||||||||||||||||||||||||||||||||||||||||||||||||||||||||||||||||||||||||||

2

God IS Powerful

The next time you are in a position where you can either stand up or walk away, use the power God has given to you.

WHEN WE ARE BORN, we do not yet understand what it means to exist. We become part of an established world that we do not know. We need our parents or guardians to care for us and teach us.

Somehow, somewhere along the way, we forget that each one of us was created for a special purpose in life. *We also forget that God has given each one of us great power.*

In chapter 4 of the book of Esther, we learn the story of Queen Esther. Queen Esther was married to a very prominent king and her position as his wife came with much power. In fact, the queen had the ability to save lives. However, she was unaware of her position of power.

One day, the queen received a disturbing message from a relative concerning the intended annihilation of her generation. Her relative reminded her of her position. He expressed to her the seriousness of the matter and asked her to consider what it might be like to never see one's family again. He asked her to think about how devastating it would be for so many to die. After realizing how dire the situation was, Queen Esther took action on behalf of her people. She approached the King and beseeched him to take action. In the end, she helped save many people's lives.

Just imagine what would have happened if the queen had not used her royal position. Just imagine what would have happened if she had not realized how mighty the position was that God had given her. Many of us are afraid to move forward and go beyond where we are told we can go. We forget that, if we just take one step with faith, we are using the power that God has given us. Like Queen Esther, we can use our God-given power to do great things, if only we recognize how we have been blessed.

Do you understand your position? The great God we serve has given you great power. You can use that power no matter where you are in life.

The next time you are in a position where you can either stand up or walk away, take a leap of faith and take action. Use the power God has given to you.

Who knows? Perhaps you have come to royal dignity for just such a time as this.

Esther 4:14

3

God IS Shelter in a Storm

Once, I found myself in a storm. Finally, I found a resting place: I looked to God. I was in the calm in the eye of the storm.

WHEN WE ARE FACED WITH challenges and we encounter trying circumstances, it can feel like a storm in our lives. Of course, like storms, these hard times come and go. But when we are in the midst of them and so much seems impossible, we often need help. I have heard that the safest place to be during a storm is in its "eye," the calm place at the storm's center. So it is with God and His presence in our lives during difficult times.

Once, I found myself in a storm—a troublesome time in my life. I was not prepared for this storm; I was not sheltered.

I could not see, and the storm obscured my vision. As days went by and the storm continued, it seemed as though it would never stop. The more I tried to lift my legs to walk, the harder it became. I felt hopeless.

Finally, I found a resting place: *I looked to God.* Suddenly, life became bearable. With God, I was in the calm in the eye of the storm. God, in His greatness, was able to give me peace that surpassed my own understanding. The storm winds still surrounded me, but I was safe in God's hands. When the storm had passed, I had a new life and a new home. I was in one place when the storm began and in another, better place when the storm ended.

Even when times are hard, God would never leave us, nor would He forsake us.

God is great. He can calm any storm in our lives, if we only trust Him.

. . . he made the storm be still, and the waves of the sea were hushed.

Psalm 107:29

4

God IS Committed to You

Some times in our lives will be harder than others. Let us remember that God can guide us, and let us be true to our commitment to Him, as He is to us.

I F I HAVE LEARNED ANYTHING over the course of my life, I have learned that God is committed to me.

Not long ago, my husband and I began a church. We had been living a life in devotion to God for over 20 years, but starting a church was a new level of commitment for us. Soon, God elevated me to the position of pastor. Both of my parents were there to witness this auspicious occasion. I felt I had accomplished a great thing in my life: I was able to make my father and mother proud of me.

Soon after starting the church, we received a report that my dad had myeloma cancer. This cancer took root in the bone of his leg. It was strange to me, but I thought to myself, "We can get through this." The issue seemed small, for I had faith in God that He would be there for my father. I looked at the situation and said, "Dad will be able to come through this and proclaim the healing of the Lord! So many will be encouraged by the difficult trial he will overcome."

But my dad's fight was not an easy one. There were up days and down days. There were days when I would visit him and it was as if no bad news had ever come to us. He smiled when he saw me, and the room lit up with his joy. But then there were the down days when my father was not doing well. On those days, I questioned God. On those days I said, "God where are you? You are taking too long to deliver him." As time passed and things seemed more dim, I even thought, *God, now this is ridiculous.*

I wanted my father to get better. At night, I dreamed of a miracle. The dream was so real. I believed it. We even sang about it in church.

One day, I had to take a deep breath, hold my heart, and really acknowledge for the first time the possibility of my father leaving me. Suddenly I had to experience my relationship with Christ in a different way: in the context of life and death. I didn't want my father to die. For the first time, I questioned my life of devotion to Christ. All I had known was trust in God. All I had known was a life devoted to God. I was faltering, and the pain was unbearable. I cried as I walked through this journey.

But then I remembered I had made a commitment to God—and He had made a commitment to me. I could not turn back. I had to walk with the great God, the great God I knew. As I did so, God began to remind me of what He had already brought me through. I remembered God would never leave me, nor would He forsake me. Nothing would separate me from the love of God. I remembered words in the book of Romans (8:38–39):

> For I am sure that neither death, nor life, nor angels, nor principalities, nor things present, nor things to come, nor powers, nor height, nor depth, nor any thing else in all creation, will be able to separate us from the love of Go in Christ Jesus our Lord.

I began to speak what I knew to be true. I accepted what was a reality. The life that my father lived on earth was coming to an end. More times than we care to admit, we hold on to what we care about so much that we fail to recognize that if we let go, we will free the person—and ourselves.

I cherished each day of the remainder of my father's life. The week of his departure, my dad lifted up his hand and waved to me as I was entering the room. I knew he was saying hello and goodbye all at the same time. That moment made an everlasting imprint on my life. *Farewell, my wonderful father.*

My dad has passed on. He lived a good life, and his spirit and his legacy will be forever remembered and have a lasting impact on the lives that he has touched. Through his passing, my life has taken on a new level of devotion, and my purpose is even more illuminated.

Some times in our lives will be harder than others. Let us be mindful to keep the great God we serve in the center of our existence. Let us be true to our commitment to Him, as He is committed to us. Then He will guide us through the difficult times.

When the righteous cry for help, the Lord hears, and rescues them from all their troubles.

Psalm 34:17

5

God IS a Keeper of Promises

We have the promises of God to comfort us in our weakest moments. With God, everyone has the ability to achieve and accomplish great things.

THE PROMISES OF GOD ARE REAL.

Our God is a God that does not go back on His word. The promises that He gives to us are given with assurance. We can rely on them when we are fearful and doubtful.

I would like to share one young woman's story. She was a single mother with four children. This woman loved God with all of her heart. But she often found herself feeling overwhelmed. With no husband to help, she struggled to make ends meet for her family. Limited by her education, she was unable to pursue a decent job. She began to question the choices she had made in her life. She wondered if she should not have had children. This thought consumed her every day.

The temptation to give up was so strong. Most mornings were a constant battle of fear, doubt, disappointment, and despair. There were times when no one seemed to want to listen.

Still, she prayed, seeking God for refuge from her struggles.

One day while praying, she heard the voice of the Lord say to her, "You can do it!" Suddenly, things clicked into place. She began to look past what was in front of her. She sought out ways to better her situation.

With her trust in God, she went back to school and completed her associates degree in human resources. Today she has a full-time job, and she is proud of her ability support her family.

When we pray, we should not doubt the promises of God. We should never feel anxious that God will not fulfill His promises.

Life often throws curve balls at us. We must learn how to deal with them. But we have God on our side. We have the promises of God to comfort us in our weakest moments. Remember this, and remind yourself that with God, everyone has the ability to achieve and accomplish great things.

God loves us. He always keeps His promises.

Trust in the Lord with all your heart, and do not rely on your own insight. In all your ways acknowledge him, and he will make straight your paths.

Proverbs 3:5–6

6

God IS Almighty

God's power rules over the frailty of man. Trust God in His almighty power!

O H, HOW MARVELOUS TO KNOW that our God is strong and almighty. His strength goes beyond that of a knight in shining armor rescuing a damsel in distress. It goes beyond anything we can imagine.

God's incredible power means that when God makes a promise to you, the possibilities know no bounds. His is a promise that goes beyond what we can see.

Our eyes are limited to believing in only the things put before us; but it is through the faith in our hearts that we witness God's incredible promises.

I am reminded of a story in the Bible about one of God's most remarkable promises. In the book of Genesis, we learn the story of God and Abraham. God promised Abraham that if he would follow Him and keep His commands, then God would bless Abraham and his future generations and bring Abraham a child. Now, keep in mind that at the time God made this promise, Abraham was 99 years of age. At that age most of us wouldn't be able to say, "I believe You, God." It takes at least a couple "hits over the head" for us to recognize that God is the head of our life and He knows what's best for us—and if we haven't had those realizations by the time we are 99, it's hard to believe we ever could.

But this was not the case for Abraham. He believed.

God can bring about events that no man could ever dream of. Sure enough, Abraham and his wife Sarah were promised a son, and God proved true to His promise. Their son Isaac was born.

God's power rules over the frailty of man. Trust God in His almighty power.

...I am God Almighty; walk before me, and be blameless.

Genesis 17:1

7

God IS Love

God's love is unconditional. It looks beyond the errors
of our ways and seeks to make our lives abundant.
Let us do the same for others.

THE WORD "LOVE" MEANS something different to each
one of us. In fact, in the Greek language, there are many
different words for "love." *Eros* is romantic love. When we
think of falling in love or meeting our true love, we are thinking of eros. A love for a place, a thing, or a special interest or
hobby is expressed by the word *philos,* meaning "love of." But
the greatest of all love is unconditional love, known as *agape.*
Unconditional love is a love that will never falter or cease. It is
totally selfless; whether the love one gives is returned or not,
that person continues to love, without any benefit to oneself.

This is the love that God has for us.

We learn of God's unconditional love in chapter 15 of the book of Luke, in the story of the prodigal son. This story is an example of unconditional love in action, explained for us so we can understand it. In this story, a father has two sons. The youngest of the two decides it is his time to leave home and make his own way in the world. He demands that his inheritance be paid to him early, and he proceeds to leave with the money. It doesn't take long for him to waste the funds. A famine strikes the city where he lives, and he soon finds himself with nothing. The young man is forced to eat the very food he had been feeding to the swine. He realizes his only hope is to return home.

The young man expects to be scolded and shamed by his family upon his return. His greatest hope is that he be allowed to stay and work amongst the hired servants. But when he arrives, his family greets him with joy.

Luke 15:20–24 relates the story:

So he set off and went to his father. But while he was still far off, his father saw him and was filled with compassion; he ran and put his arms around him and kissed him. Then the son said to him, "Father, I have sinned against heaven and before you; I am no longer worthy to be called your son." But the father said to his slaves, "Quickly, bring out a robe—the best one—and put it on him. . . let us eat and celebrate; for this son of mine was dead and is alive again; he was lost and is found!"

The young man's family had thought he was lost or dead, and they were overjoyed to see that he was alive and healthy. Despite his wrongdoings and his past mistakes, his family welcomed the young man back with open arms.

Although he had made mistakes and hurt his family, the prodigal son was welcomed back with love. This is the meaning of unconditional love, and this is the love that God has for his children. Although we may stray from God, He will always welcome us back with open arms.

God also desires for us to share this kind of love with each other. Let us not be so quick to harbor hostility toward someone else—for we never know when we will need total love and acceptance extended to us.

God's love looks beyond the errors of our ways and seeks to make our lives abundant. Let us share this same spirit of love with others.

And we have known and believed the love that God hath to us. God is love; and he that dwelleth in love dwelleth in God, and God in him.

1 John 4:16

---

ll

"Open your hearts to the love God instills…God loves you tenderly. What He gives you is not to be kept under lock and key, but to be shared."

—Mother Teresa

llllllllllllllllllllllllllllllllllllllllllllllllllllllllllllllllllllllllllllllllllllllll

8

God IS Loving Kindness

As we empty ourselves out, giving love to others, we allow God to fill us with His spirit. Loving others presents us with the opportunity to allow the love of God to shine through us.

OUR LOVE OF GOD COMES with a commitment. We can't hate our brother or sister and say we love God. We have a commitment to value each other the same way that God values us. This means we must offer unconditional love to others, love that is totally selfless. We must give our love to another person, even if this act does not benefit us in any way.

We can find someone who needs our love everywhere we look.

I remember riding home on the subway one day. I was consumed with thoughts of my daily tasks and the bills I needed to pay, calculating the cost of each and trying to balance the books in my head. As the train stopped at one station, I happened to notice as a young lady entered the train. She was burdened with a large black garbage bag and a broom. She also held the hands of two small children who were so young they could barely walk. As I watched this young lady press her way through the crowd, moving forward despite her burden, I realized that moments before I had felt just as burdened as she. I couldn't believe I had been so consumed by mere thoughts! Something so much more important was before me. I did not know who this woman was, and I did not know her situation. I only knew what I saw: a fellow person, a sister, in need. Suddenly, my heart melted. *This young lady needed help.* I could feel this with such certainty.

Yet I did not know how I could help her, especially when I only had five dollars in my pocket. What could I offer her?

At the next stop, she began to prepare to exit the train. Suddenly, I felt compelled to give her my last. I walked up to her and said, "Excuse me, I don't know you, but would you take this money?" I pressed the five-dollar bill into her hand. She looked at me, and I saw she was so grateful that she had tears in her eyes.

I don't know who was serviced more that day, the young lady or me. As I made my way home, I too had tears in my eyes; but I felt so fulfilled. I had no money in my pocket, yet I felt like a million dollars. I wanted to shout it out. I wanted to share with everyone that I had obeyed the voice of God.

Love does not ask questions or expect anything in return; it looks beyond the divide between us and sees the need. Although I did not know the woman on the train, I could see that she had a need greater than my own.

In 1 Corinthians 13:3, the Bible tells us:

If I give away all my possessions, and if I hand over my body so that I may boast, but do not have love, I gain nothing.

As we empty ourselves out, giving love to others, we allow God to fill us with His spirit. Loving others presents us with the opportunity to allow the love of God to shine through us.

Every day, we have a choice. We can sacrifice our own desires for the good of someone else. In reaching out to others like this, we reach out with gratitude toward the God who first loved us.

Beloved, let us love one another, because love is from God; everyone who loves is born of God, and knows God.

1 John 4:7

"Faith is taking the first step even when you don't see the whole staircase."

—Martin Luther King, Jr.

9

God IS a Provider

We are rich when we recognize the power of God. You have God to rely on when troubles come into your life.

WHEN WE HEAR A STORY of someone else's good fortune, sometimes we cannot help feeling doubtful that God would do the same for us. We can believe in the power of God and the will of God for other people, but when it comes to our own lives, we dismiss God's abilities.

It is like we have shut God away and placed Him in a box.

This is especially true when times are tough. But it is not wise to forget God's power. We have Him to rely on as we go through life.

Take a moment to think about how God has fulfilled His promises to you. Think about how He has provided for you.

When we think about being provided for, food and other necessities come to mind. For most of us, these needs are fulfilled through the jobs we have. But we do not rely on ourselves alone. It is God that allowed each one of us to obtain those jobs. It is God that provided an open door for you to walk through.

When we lose a job, we can become angry. We may even blame God. But let us be careful how we minimize the greatness of God. The God that provided a job for you is the same God that will provide a way for you to survive without that job.

The Bible asks us this: If God will provide for the birds in the air, what more will He do for you?

As Matthew 6:26 tells us,

> *Look at the birds of the air; they neither sow nor reap nor gather into barns, and yet your heavenly Father feeds them. Are you not of more value than they?*

In Matthew 6:31–33, the Bible also tells us to remember what is truly important: abundance of spirit.

> *Therefore do not worry, saying, "What will we eat?" or "What will we drink?" or "What will we wear?" For it is the Gentiles who strive for all these things; and indeed your heavenly Father knows that you need all these things. But strive first for the kingdom of God and his*

righteousness, and all these things will be given to you as well.

We are rich when we recognize the power of God. God loves you, and He has made promises to you. He will fulfill them. Hold this certainty close to your heart.

You have God to rely on when troubles come into your life.

So do not worry about tomorrow, for tomorrow will bring worries of its own. Today's trouble is enough for today.

Matthew 6:34

||||||||||||||||||||||||||||||||||||||||||||||||||||||||||||||||||||||||||||||||||||||||||||||

"God has given us two hands, one to receive with and
the other to give with."

—Reverend Billy Graham

||||||||||||||||||||||||||||||||||||||||||||||||||||||||||||||||||||||||||||||||||||||||||||||

10

God IS
Compassionate

Our God is compassionate. Let's show the same
compassion toward each other.

WHEN I WAS A CHILD, I always wondered why I saw
people sleeping outside on the streets. Why were they
sleeping in cardboard boxes when I could look up and see
so many buildings that could shelter them? *Why can't these
people just live in those buildings*, I thought to myself.

Of course, children have no concept of the actual cost of
living. All children know is that we exist and life should be
beautiful. They don't yet understand that we must obtain an
education to get a good job, so we can earn enough money
to acquire the basic necessities. As a child witnessing people
on the streets, all I could think about was how I would like

to help them. One day, I was certain, I would have so much money that no one would live on the streets. As far-fetched as it sounds, that was the measure of compassion that I had in my heart as a little girl.

As adults, we may sometimes find ourselves looking down on individuals who don't have what we have. When this occurs, it means we have lost our sense of compassion for others. We do not realize that when we lose our sense of compassion, we diminish the power we have to make a difference in others' lives.

Our God is merciful and compassionate. Consider this the next time you pass by someone who has no home or food.

Compassion is your heart's treasure, and no one should ever take it from you. Compassion flows from the heart, and assisting others through your heart of compassion is your greatest gift. In your heart, propose to do a good deed every day for someone less fortunate than you. Our God seeks ways to bless us; let's do the same for our neighbors.

God is great.

But you, O Lord, are a God merciful and gracious, slow to anger and abounding in steadfast love and faithfulness.

Psalm 86:15

11

God IS Omnipresent

God will always be wherever I go. God commands
His whole creation; there is no corner in which He is
absent. Try as I might, I can never escape Him. This
thought comforts me.

IN THIS DAY AND AGE, WE ARE all being watched at some
point and time. Video cameras film us as we exit and enter
stores, and our cell phone signals tell people where we were
and when we are there. It can seem that we are being followed,
in one way or another, every day of our lives. In fact, this is
true. The great God we serve is always watching out for us.

If we were to fly at the speed of light from one side of
the sky to the other, we still could not escape the presence
of God. No matter how distant the horizon, we will always

find that God is already there. Geography cannot separate us from God! Neither can space or time. Some may think, "If I could just leave this planet and journey to a distant solar system, then I would no longer be accountable to God." Or, "If I could just travel through time to the past or the future, then I would no longer be answerable to God." But man is always accountable to God, everywhere and anywhere, for God is not bound by space or time.

One reason why God is so near to us is because He created us. God gave us life and He knows how we think and work. God did not merely create us and then let us go. God is always thinking about you and me. He cares deeply for us, and we are in his thoughts at every moment. When I think that such a powerful God is looking down on me and cheering for me, I am filled with awe.

We may forget about God, or cease to think about him at certain moments. But God *never* forgets about us.

At one point or another, all of us feel the need to run far away from life. But because a great God cares for us, there is no escape from His love and protection. Even if we are in a distant land far away from home, far away from family at college, traveling all alone, or serving in the military in a war-torn country, we are no further away from God and His protection.

In a sense, everywhere and every place is home because God is there.

. . . though indeed he is not far from each one of us. For "In him we live and move and have our being. . . "

Acts of the Apostles 17:27–28

12

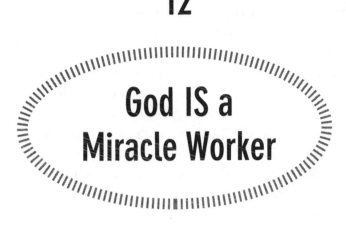

God IS a
Miracle Worker

God works His miracles in cooperation with His people.
He wants us involved. He wants us to be active.

WHEN WE HEAR ABOUT MIRACLES happening, many of us often wonder, "Why have they not yet happened to me?"

The truth is, miracles happen for us all the time. We just need to receive them.

We learn about receiving miracles in the scriptures. Mark 6:35–44 tells us the story of Jesus feeding thousands of the hungry from only a small portion of bread and fish. When the story takes place, Jesus had just finished preaching to a crowd of 5,000 men. The Bible recounts that when it started to get late, Jesus' disciples came to him because they were concerned that the crowd needed to eat.

The Bible says in Mark 6:35-37:

When it grew late, his disciples came to him and said, "This is a deserted place, and the hour is now very late; send them away so that they may go into the surrounding country and villages and buy something for themselves to eat." But he answered them, "You give them something to eat." They said to him, "Are we to go and buy two hundred denarii worth of bread, and give it to them to eat?"

I love Jesus's reply: "You give them something to eat." Wow! When his disciples came to Jesus, they probably expected him to have those folks in the crowd sent away so they could eat on their own. Instead, he asked that the disciples take action. I can imagine them saying, "Excuse me? How do you expect us to do this? There are thousands of people out there! Just the cooking itself would take months between the twelve of us. The cost would be at least 8 months of wages. This is impossible! *Jesus, are you serious?"*

The story continues with Jesus asking his disciples how much food they have on hand. "How many loaves do you have?" he asks. He directs them to find out: "Go and see."

The Bible continues in Mark 6:38–44:

When they had found out, they said, "Five, and two fish." Then he ordered them to get all the people to sit down in groups on the green grass. So they sat down in groups of hundreds and of fifties. Taking the five loaves and the two fish, he looked up to heaven, and blessed and broke the loaves, and gave them to his disciples to set before the people; and he divided the two fish among them all. And all ate and were filled; and they took up twelve baskets full of broken pieces and of the fish. Those who had eaten the loaves numbered five thousand men.

If you think about it, the number was probably even greater than 5,000. Those men, hearing that Jesus was there, probably took their families with them. With their wives and children (probably many children—believe me, they did not limit themselves to two or three children in those days!), there may have been at least 25,000 people in that crowd. What a miracle!

How can we bring such miracles into our lives?

One of the first things we must do is ask for help. *If you want something to be given to you, ask. It's that simple.*

Another thing we must do is recognize our own power. Even the disciples made the mistake of forgetting their own resourcefulness. We can utilize what we already have. We can take action. This is why Jesus said to his disciples, "How many loaves do you have?" and "Go and see."

God works His miracles in cooperation with His people. He wants us involved. He wants us to be active. Throughout the Bible it is apparent that God rarely acts alone but instead acts in cooperation with us. Some would rather wait in their houses, waiting for God's miracle in their lives. They prefer to mumble, "Why does God not answer me?" My friends, He wants you to be involved with Him. He wants your cooperation. Why? Because it will help you develop a relationship with God. *God is a God of relationships, not a genie that you can keep in a bottle.*

You may wonder, "But what can I give God in return?" Ask God. Work on your relationship with Him. He will let you know. It may be that He wants you to go to a church that believes in God's miracles. Or it may be to reach out to others to heal them. Ask Him. He will let you know.

God is great. He makes great miracles.

The plans of the mind belong to mortals, but the answer of the tongue is from the Lord.

Proverbs 16:1

13

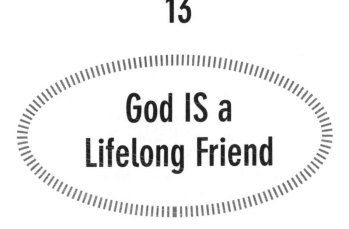

God IS a Lifelong Friend

God lets us know that our relationship with Him is far greater than any relationship with any man or woman here on earth. It is our responsibility to be subject to the hand of God in our lives.

OUR RELATIONSHIP WITH GOD is far more rich and enduring than any other.

I'm reminded of a story of a friend of mine. Although she had two parents in her life whom she loved, she grew up without having her biological father present. She longed greatly for him. Her identity seemed to be somehow lost without his presence. As she grew into a young woman, it was hard for her to make the right choices concerning men in her life. She often chose relationships that were not good for her. She couldn't see the danger ahead.

She did not know that she was falling head on into the traps of the adversary. But despite this, the young woman was also involved in a relationship with someone more powerful than any man she had ever met: God.

For years, the young woman endured a painful relationship with one young man in particular. She suffered through betrayal and hurt. Her friends and family were so frustrated. It seemed nothing could pull her away from this man. But one day, a fire struck her family's home. The damage caused was irrevocable and the family had to move.

After the move, the relationship completely dissolved. Not long after, the young woman received news that the man she had been dating had become physically violent. She realized that if she had stayed in the relationship, she herself could have been hurt. She felt very fortunate. She remembered the word of God in Proverbs 3:5–6: "Trust in the Lord with all your heart. . . and he will make straight your paths." If it had not been for the fire, this young woman would be with that young man to this day.

God lets us know that our relationship with Him is far greater than any relationship with any man or woman here on earth. It is our responsibility to be subject to the hand of God in our lives.

Now we have received not the spirit of the world, but the Spirit that is from God, so that we may understand the gifts bestowed on us by God.

1 Corinthians 2:12

VICTORIOUS

Let the soldiers of the Lord blow the trumpet
Let the people rejoice, for we are victorious

Just lift your voice in victory
No matter what it looks like, you are not defeated
Just let it ring out like a trumpet

—from the song written and composed by
  Pastor Darren Jenkins

III

"All I have seen teaches me to trust the Creator for all I have not seen."

—Ralph Waldo Emerson

IIIIIIIIIIIIIIIIIIIIIIIIIIIIIIIIIIIIIIIIIIIIIIIIIIIIIIIIIIIIIIIIIIIIIIIIIIIIIIIIIIIIIIIIIIIIIIIIIII

14

God IS Your Conductor

God does not give us superficial ideas or dreams. Take your dream to God so that He can develop and guide you.

I**T'S HARD TO FIND YOURSELF** in the world that we live in.

We live in such a competitive society. Most people are living to reach what they have been told is "the top." Trying to compete under these circumstances can be exhausting. It seems easier to give up rather than to persevere.

It's funny that we place our hands in the hands of man to lead us to our destiny, but we can't trust God, who gives life to all men. It is only God who can help us find the path for our lives and who we really are.

We are so quick to overlook God's direction for us. It's like a train conductor who gives a passenger specific instructions to follow. He says, "If you follow these instructions, you will reach your destination." Why would the passenger ignore him? No one knows the schedule better than the conductor himself. Why bother to ask for the directions if you do not intend to follow them? And yet when it comes to God's direction for us, we often think we have a better plan.

Be assured that God cares for you. God does not give us superficial ideas or dreams. In other words, our dreams are not given to us for naught. However, if we do not take our dreams and plans to God so that He may develop and guide us, we are bound to err. With God, we can have full confidence in success. Psalm 27:1 reads, "The Lord is my light and my salvation; whom shall I fear? The Lord is the stronghold of my life; of whom shall I be afraid?"

Yielding all unto God brings us riches and glory and life. There is no greater happiness and security for the present and the future than knowing God.

Allow God to guide you along the path of what is good.

I believe that I shall see the goodness of the Lord in the land of the living.

Psalm 27:13

15

God IS Working for You

The tosses and turns in life can push us toward the best of times and the worst of times. But we should never forget that God always has a plan for us.

F OR MANY OF US, THE LIFE we had always imagined consists of obtaining a good education, getting a good job, starting a family, owning a home, and settling down until retirement.

Of course, we have since learned that plan is not reality for everyone.

Where we start in life is not always our end, and the tosses and turns in life can push us toward the best of times and the worst of times. But we should never forget that God always has a plan for us.

The Bible promises us in Philipians 1:6, "... the one who began a good work among you will bring it to completion by the day of Jesus Christ." God has invested His love in us. When our lives do not go as we had planned, we can lose sight of this. Remember, though, that a house is merely wood, plaster, and bricks before it is completed. A plan has to be thought out and established, and a location has to be chosen. God is working on all of this for us. Although our lives may at times seem like rubble, they are in fact works in progress. God is building a future for us.

As disorganized as our lives may seem, we must realize that if God places a desire and a dream within you, it is He that will provide the necessary tools.

In all that we deal with every day of our lives, we can be assured that God has an expected path for our lives. It's up to us to receive the offer and live according to His plan.

Commit your work to the Lord, and your plans will be established.

Proverbs 16:3

16

God IS There for You to Trust

We should not allow others to tell us what we can or will become. Instead, we must follow God. We have not really lived a fulfilling life until we have placed our trust in the hands of God.

HAVE YOU EVER FELT OUT of control of your own life? Has it ever seemed like people were constantly telling you what you should do and how to do it? Sometimes we can feel like we are living through others' dreams or aspirations for us. Under these circumstances it can be extremely difficult to choose a vocation that fits us.

We should not allow others to tell us what we can or will become. Instead, we must follow God. Developing a relationship with God is imperative. *Ask yourself, who is the head of your life: Is it man or is it God?*

I am reminded of a young woman who desperately desired to dance. As a young child her greatest dream was to be a dancer. She participated in all the dance programs in school and within the community. Sadly, her parents never seemed to have the time to come to the shows she participated in. The little girl had other siblings who pursued athletics, and it seemed they received more attention.

After realizing that dancing was really and truly her passion, the young lady decided to talk to her mom. She came to her mother with fire in her eyes and a heart filled with desperate hope that her desire would be accepted. But mother calmly replied, "There is no real hope in dance, and there's no money in dance." Her mom insisted that the passion her daughter felt so greatly was only an infatuation and that it would soon pass.

Well, it was not an infatuation, and the passion has remained. Now 40, this woman still dreams of dancing on stage one day. She longs to perform just one dance with the Alvin Ailey American Dance Theater.

Let us not place our dreams in someone else's hands, and let us be careful of who we share our dreams with. *There are many who can't see what you see.* They are limited to what society has shown them. They are cautious, and they don't believe in how far they will go in life. It is like they can only walk the fine line along the perimeter of possibility. But when we place our lives in the hand of God, our expectations can be as great as we dream.

I implore you to live the best life you can for the rest of your life. Do not compromise the things of importance to you; trust in who you are. When we are at one with God, what is the worst thing that can happen to us if we fall? The answer is that we will fall into His hands, and He will catch us. The only assurance we have is the trust we put in God. Our God is not a God of chance. When He makes us a promise, He does not risk our life in a game of chance. You can rest assured that His promises are real.

We have not really lived a fulfilling life until we have placed our trust in the hands of God. He will guide us through every step of the way, if we allow Him to. Move forward on faith, build a lasting relationship with God, and pursue your dreams.

May the glory of the Lord endure forever; may the Lord rejoice in His works.

Psalm 104:31

"Nor shall derision prove powerful against those who listen to humanity or those who follow in the footsteps of divinity, for they shall live forever. Forever."

—Khalil Gibran, "The Voice of the Poet"

17

God IS Your Direction

Since a man is unable to fully understand God's purpose in our life, he has to walk by faith. This can be so hard. But do not give up. Seek God and follow His direction.

A S WE GO THROUGH LIFE, we are often tempted to move in the wrong direction. We may inwardly hear the voice of the Lord telling us to go one way, but we may choose the opposite direction from what God tells us because the other way looks a little more colorful and lively. *Listening to sound direction is one of the hardest things for a human to do.*

How many times have we witnessed the downfall of so-called great leaders? It's hard for human beings to accept that less is greater than more. This is one of the reasons why we see "great" people fall from grace. They excelled to the top, and then because of greed and neglect of what is right, they hit the bottom—hard.

I'm reminded of a story in the book of Judges concerning Samson. God had given Samson a limitless source of strength. With God's strength, Samson's power was insurmountable, and he could defeat any enemy.

But then Samson began to act irresponsibly.

The first sign of trouble was Samson's lack of obedience to his parents. He also showed disrespect for religious tradition. Worse of all, Samson was overcome by the beauty and appeal of a woman named Delilah. Samson let down his guard and was weakened by Delilah. Delilah used this to her advantage and stole Samson's source of strength from him by clipping his hair. Without God's strength, Samson was easily captured by the enemy. Humiliated, he was forced to work in an arena for the amusement of crowds of people.

God did not make us robots. He gave us our own free will to make decisions about our lives. Still, it is equally important that we acknowledge God's role in the direction we choose to follow. Since a man is unable to fully understand God's purpose in his life, he has to walk with faith. This can be so hard. But do not give up.

God does not look for us to fail. He has our best interest at heart and He wants us to succeed. When we are able to follow the truths of God and guard His wisdom, then God Himself will prove to be effective in our lives.

Seek God and follow His direction. Stick to the plan that He has for your life. God will never leave us without direction if we seek Him.

No testing has overtaken you that is not common to everyone. God is faithful, and he will not let you be tested beyond your strength, but with the testing he will also provide the way out so that you may be able to endure it.

1 Corinthians 10:13

II

"Whoever possesses God in their being, has him in
a divine manner, and he shines out to them in all
things; for them all things taste of God and in all
things it is God's image that they see."

—Meister Eckhart

IIIIIIIIIIIIIIIIIIIIIIIIIIIIIIIIIIIIIIIIIIIIIIIIIIIIIIIIIIIIIIIIIIIIIIIIIIIIIIIIIIIIIIIIIIIIII

18

God IS a Teacher

Sometimes it takes the hearts of others to reveal to us the errors of our ways.

THERE ARE MANY OF US who walk through this life feeling that we are not accountable for our behavior. We somehow forget that for every action, there is a reaction.

Sometimes we can become so deeply involved in something that wrong becomes right to us, and we forget the errors of our ways. This is when a new perspective can help us. Sometimes this new perspective comes from others.

Psalm 51 tells us the story of King David. King David had a prominent position, but like many leaders, he let the prestige and job status get the best of him. He did a terrible thing that affected many lives and caused great pain.

Unfortunately, even after recognizing that what he had done was wrong, King David continued to try to fix the matter in his own way. This only led to worse extremes, causing even more death and heartache.

A different perspective was necessary to make King David see the light. The Bible tells us of a man who came to King David and offered to tell the king a story of a man who had done great wrongs. After hearing the story, King David was shocked that the man in the tale had committed such awful acts. The king thought that what the man had done was unforgivable and that this person should be put to death.

Isn't it funny how we can judge someone else, yet fail to recognize our own mistakes?

When King David asked the storyteller who the man in the story was, the storyteller revealed that the man was in fact King David himself. When the King learned this, he was sorrowful in his heart. King David then made a plea unto the Lord in a prayer of repentance. He sought forgiveness for his wrongdoing from God.

Once sincerity was in Kind David's heart, God forgave him.

Remember to be aware of how your actions affect others. Sometimes, someone else will reveal this to you; God often brings people into our lives as a means to teach us. God can use anyone for this purpose. Once you learn of your wrongdoing, turn to God for forgiveness.

. . . for wisdom will come into your heart, and knowledge will be pleasant to your soul; prudence will watch over you; and understanding will guard you.

Proverbs 2:10-11

19

God IS Benevolent

We are all bound to make mistakes. Extend kindness, understanding, and forgiveness to those around you.

W E HAVE ALL SINNED AND fallen short of the glory of God. The good news is that that we have done nothing so terrible that God will not forgive us. *We can go to God and ask Him to forgive us and He will.* God does not intend that we should be tormented by our errors. In fact, God is eager to forgive us.

We should do the same for one another.

I am reminded of a story in the Bible from Matthew 18:21–33. In this story, a young man had great debt. The debt collector came to retrieve the amount of money owed to him. The young man pleaded for mercy. He begged for more time.

He had nothing to offer to clear his balance. The debt collector said that he would forgive him and cancel the debt owed. The young man could now live in peace.

Soon after, the young man encountered someone who owed him money. This person owed an amount that was less than the young man had owed not long ago. But the young man forgot the compassion and mercy that had been offered to him. Instead, he threatened the man and threw him in jail. But then the good deed bestowed on the young man was reversed, and he was put in jail until his debt was paid in full.

God is the ultimate forgiving God. If we open our hearts to forgive others, God will do the same for us. Matthew 6:14-15 tells us, "For if you forgive others their trespasses, your heavenly Father will also forgive you; but if you do not forgive others, neither will your Father forgive your trespasses."

Remember, not one of us is perfect, and we are all bound to make mistakes. Extend kindness, understanding, and forgiveness to those around you.

Little children, let us love, not in word or speech, but in truth and action.

1 John 3:18

20

God IS Forgiving

God told us to love one another and to forgive one another. Learn to forgive everyone in your life, even if it is challenging.

GOD KNOWS THAT FORGIVENESS is the only way we can live our lives together.

In the Bible the disciples ask, "Lord, if another member of the church sins against me, how often should I forgive?" Jesus' reply was "Not seven times, but, I tell you, seventy-seven times" (Matthew 18:21–22), which means there should be no limit to how often we forgive someone.

Of course, it is easy to *say* that we love God and we love his people. But acting on that is another thing altogether—especially when the person who has hurt us is someone we are close to, like a friend, family member, or spouse.

Why is it so hard to forgive in a marriage? It can seem easier to forgive those we don't know. Is it because we have not witnessed all of a stranger's errors firsthand? We often take the time to counsel and pray with a stranger and encourage him or her to stay strong. *But oftentimes the last thing in the world we are willing to do is forgive a partner for something he or she has done.*

My husband and I have been married for 21 years (wow). We got married at a very young age. At the time, we did not know much. All we knew was that we were in love and wanted to live our lives together. After being married for a little over a year, we began to really learn about one another. We began to realize that some of our marriage's issues existed as the result of the baggage we were both bringing with us into our new, shared life "as one." Each suitcase was filled with our own ideas, past experiences, problems, hang-ups—the list went on and on. But the important lesson we learned is that, if we had not learned how to forgive one another for things we said or did, our marriage would have failed before it had really gotten started.

God told us to love one another and to be forgiving of one another. Learn to forgive those in your life so that you may be able to live happily and love the people closest to you.

Create in me a clean heart, O God, and put a new and right spirit within me.

Psalm 51

21

God IS
Open-Hearted

Free yourself from the burden of bitter feelings toward other people. Think of how much more pleasant our world would be if we were to have forgiving hearts. God is willing to forgive you unconditionally; can you do the same?

IT BAFFLES ME TO THINK we live in a world that has the mentality of "an eye for an eye and a tooth for a tooth" when we have such a faithful God who is so wise and caring. God does not want us to carry grudges.

Most people hold on to a wrong that has been dealt to them. When they do this and become angry at other people, they allow themselves to be visited by pain, hurt, fragility, and constant discomfort. It's amazing to me how people repeat the old cliché "I'll forgive you, but I will not forget." This is not forgiveness!

We must realize that each individual has to deal with all types of challenges, and to refuse extending forgiveness to another merely adds yet another challenge to that person's life. To go forward without being forgiven is a heavy weight that none of us should ever have to carry.

Free yourself from the burdens of bitter feelings toward people in your life. God does not hold grudges against you, so don't hold any against another. *Be free.* Holding on to a wrong done to you will only cause anger and hostility. Taking time to erase the bitterness in our hearts is far more rewarding than each day piling on remembrances of what caused bitterness. One of the greatest tools Jesus has given us in the power of prayer. Use prayer as a means to talk things over with God, and yourself. Work through your feelings. This may take awhile, but don't give up. Use prayer like a roadmap as you journey through the rough terrain of your hurt feelings. Eventually, you will arrive at forgiveness. *Use the power of prayer to help you forgive.*

Just think about how much more pleasant our world would be if we were to have forgiving hearts toward all men. God is willing to forgive you unconditionally; can you do the same?

Remember, now is the time to forgive. Tomorrow is not promised to any of us. Don't waste time being angry. Choose to be free.

. . . and be kind to one another, tender-hearted, forgiving one another, as God in Christ has forgiven you.

Ephesians 4:32

22

God IS Wise

God is great in every aspect of life. There is nothing
too hard for God.

I AM THE PROUD MOTHER OF THREE beautiful children.
Yet, some days I am amazed that someone like me could
possibly have brought these people into the world and suc-
cessfully cared for them.

The deliveries of my children were amazing. With fear
and trembling in my heart, each experience of bringing them
into the world was the most awesome experience I have
encountered.

Each one of my deliveries was unique in its own way. My
first daughter, Nicole, had to be delivered through emergency
cesarean section because her heartbeat was faint and she was

in fetal distress. My son Darren Jr. was also delivered through cesarean section; he went into fetal distress, and due to the severity of the distress, he was considered a premature delivery. Because of that, there were other complications. Darren Jr. was diagnosed with jaundice, and he had to be incubated for several days. After a continuous battery of testing, he was also diagnosed with bronchitis. In the end, though, both my children pulled through.

Now, I knew God was in my life each step of the way. However, when we are in the midst of our trying circumstances, the days seem longer, the clouds seem a little dark, and the sun just doesn't seem to shine like it should.

Not long after my second child was born, I explained to God how I wanted my life to be. My two children had come through and progressed tremendously, and I was grateful. But I did not want any more children. My plans were final. I had two children, and that was enough.

Well, God had other plans in the works. Two years later I was with child again. Oh, how devastated I was. How could this be? "God, I told you this was it for me!" I said. As time moved on, I became depressed and developed a feeling of bitterness within. I cried often and secluded myself from people. I felt embarrassment and shame because I was pregnant again. The fact that I was married did not change matters. All I could think about was the difficulties I would face having another child.

As I look back over my life, it's amazing to me how we trust God in some matters but not for all. It's like we pick and choose what we allow God to handle. We say, "Lord, you take that and I'll take this." But the truth is, what happens in life does not depend on what we can and cannot handle. In fact, our "handling" of situations usually creates havoc in our lives.

As I went through the internal struggle of not wanting another child, I began to see how selfish I was being. *Many women would love to be in my position*, I thought. I reached deep within. I began to pray for God to change my heart and my thoughts.

I remembered Psalm 34:8: "O taste and see that the Lord is good; happy are those who take refuge in Him."

I began to ask Him to take away my fear of enduring another painful delivery. Due to the fact that I had two caesarean sections, I was told I could never have a natural childbirth. I was so afraid that I would have to go through the pain of a caesarean again. I asked God to please allow me to have a natural childbirth and a healthy baby. As time went on, I treated myself better. I did things to enhance the my child's health and my own. Soon it was time for me to deliver.

Everything that could go wrong did go wrong.

The car broke down en route to the hospital, right in the middle of the road. My husband stood in the middle of traffic to hail down an ambulance. They passed us by but then turned around. Frustration and fear again threatened to grip me; but I placed my total trust in God.

I remembered Psalm 27:14: "Wait for the Lord; be strong, and let your heart take courage; wait for the Lord!"

Four hours later I delivered Brianna, a healthy, 6-pound baby girl, through natural childbirth—no medicine, no needles.

God is so good. Our thoughts, fears, and predictions are in no way comparable to God's ways and His infinite wisdom.

The Lord is good to all, and his compassion is over all that he has made.

Psalm 145:9

23

God IS Your Deliverer

No matter what the situation is, He can deliver us out
of all our troubles. How wonderful it feels to know that
we have a deliverer.

H AVE YOU EVER BEEN IN TROUBLE and needed someone to rescue you?

I can recall a time when I was stranded on the side of the
road after an axle on my car had broken. The day was rainy
and dark, and the car had shut off completely, so there was
no heat. I sat in the car, fearful, alone, and cold. Cell phones
were not as popular back then as they are today, and I had no
way to call for help.

I'm sure this story is one that many can identify with. All of us have felt abandoned and frightened at one time or another. In those moments, we imagine the worst.

As I sat in that car, every negative thought imaginable came to my mind. For some reason, the worst enters our mind before our natural instincts when we are overtaken by a sudden unwelcoming event.

Because I was fairly new to trusting in God, I took some time contemplating whether to call on Him. The storm grew more intense, and rain was pounding on the roof of the car. There was no help in sight. I realized that, alone, I could not see my way out. Finally, I began to pray and ask God to help me.

Suddenly, a knock on the door jolted me. A man was there. He asked me if I was all right. I was still afraid, so I rolled down my window just enough to tell him what had happened. He was able to help me out, and I returned home safe and sound.

How great is our God, who shows us His delivering power! No matter what the situation is, He can deliver us out of all of our troubles. How wonderful it feels to know that we have a deliverer.

The Lord is my rock, my fortress, and my deliverer. . .

Psalm 18:2

24

God IS Your Protection

The love of God surrounds us. It's a shield to protect
our hearts and a balm to heal us.

I AM REMINDED OF A STORY of a young woman who was
protected by God and who found a life in Him. This young
woman's name was Doll.

Doll was a broken girl. Her parents divorced when she
was only 2, and she greatly felt the her father's absence. When
Doll was 4, her mother remarried. A year later, so did Doll's
father. Suddenly, Doll had four parents. This was confusing
for the child. Then, when Doll was 8, she was abused by her
stepfather. The abuse continued for 5 years, and Doll was burdened with shouldering this pain by herself, in silence. Finally,
she was able to tell her mother what had been happening.

But despite the fact that she had shared the truth, Doll still felt lost.

One day, God appeared to help her. A professional football player visited Doll's school and spoke to the students. As he talked about his relationship with Jesus, everything suddenly clicked for Doll. She realized that Jesus had come to her to do what she could not do on her own. As the Bible tells us in Psalm 147:3, she felt that Jesus "came to bind up wounds and to heal my heart."

Today, Doll says that God is a constant force in her life. She says that God has been her father, her cheerleader, her friend, and her teacher. He is ever-present in her life, every day.

Doll's testimony, like others, is a story of triumph through difficult times to encourage our hearts and remind us of God's power. No matter what trials we face, difficulties will never overtake us completely because God will always protect us.

The love of God surrounds us. It's a shield to keep away feelings that can bring us fear. The winds can beat upon the shield, the rain may fall, but nothing will penetrate the protection of God.

But the Lord has become my stronghold, and my God the rock of my refuge.

Psalm 94:17–23

25

God IS
Faithful

God is true and committed in His faithfulness to us.
His faithfulness builds us up and supports us.

HAVE YOU EVER GIVEN SOMETHING to someone in
his or her time of need, only to find the favor was not
returned to you?

There have been times in my life when I went all out to
provide my gift of help to someone, and they were ungrateful.

I remember a time when I was blessed with a large
amount of money. Times were exceedingly wonderful. Then,
something strange began to happen. I suddenly started to
receive phone call after phone call, almost constantly. They
came every day, and they were always about a problem that
required a monetary supplement—from me. These people

never called for prayer or just to see how I was feeling or doing. Their conversations always had to do with meeting their financial needs.

Now, we know that people face hard times, and we must always consider how we ourselves could one day be in the same predicament. How would we want to be treated? I thought carefully about this. I was trying to be a good Christian woman and live a life of servitude. I know that God wants us to remain faithful to the end and be a help to those in need.

I asked God to search my heart and if anything was there that did not represent Him to please remove it and show me the right way. Soon after the prayer, days later, I received another dire-need phone call. But the well was dry. However, someone was in need. I offered all I could: food from my freezer and some wrapped coins worth 5 to 15 dollars. As I explained to the caller that this was all I had, they suddenly no longer wanted what I had to offer. How strange was this? What was the difference? Was it the amount or the presentation of the amount? I don't know what was different, but it felt awful because I resolved that there was not so great a need. When a person claims he is desperate and he calls for help, if the offer of help that is given is then refused, one must wonder what the true purpose was in asking.

For a while, I felt like a fool.

But then I thought about how our God is not a God that turns on and off. When we are not true and faithful to the commandments of God, He does not toss us to the side, deal with us differently, or treat us strangely. God is true and committed in His faithfulness to us. His faithfulness builds us up and supports us. True faithfulness is lasting and continuous.

In the same way that God is faithful to us, we should be faithful to Him. *We should not look to God to make a provision or meet a need, and then no longer desire a relationship with Him once He has done what we have asked.* This is also true of our relationships with one another. We can't just use people for the moment to get what we need.

One of the greatest of lessons I learned in this situation was that it doesn't matter what others do to you; it matters what you do for others. Continue to show yourself faithful in someone else's time of need. Though God may use you for a time or a season in someone's life, it is important that you retain the character of Christ. Some will follow you because of what you have, and they mean you no good; others simply need extra attention and love so they can recognize how you are sharing God's love with them. No matter what, continue to trust God, and He will reveal to you who your true friends are.

God shows His faithful love by establishing an everlasting bond with us. There is nothing too terrible that we can't be reconciled in a relationship with Him if we have gone astray.

Remember that God's faithfulness is steadfast, sure, nurturing, trustworthy, and enduring.

Know therefore that the Lord your God is God, the faithful God who maintains covenant loyalty with those who love him and keep his commandments, to a thousand generations. . .

Deuteronomy 7:9

||||||||||||||||||||||||||||||||||||||||||||||||||||||||||||||||||||||||||||||||||||||||||||||||||||||||||||

"When God calls you to do something, he enables you to do it."

—Robert Schuller

||||||||||||||||||||||||||||||||||||||||||||||||||||||||||||||||||||||||||||||||||||||||||||||||||||||||||||

26

God IS Hope

When we face reality with God's help, we feel a greater assurance that all will be well. Knowing God gives us joy.

THERE ARE TIMES IN OUR LIVES when we find our-selves at an extreme low point.

On these days, we wake with dark feelings. Some of us may rise with the fear of failure; others rise with the burden of a systematic routine weighing down their hearts. It may feel like this day is just another day in a routine, the "same old, same old." When we look at life this way, we feel hopeless. What a dreadful way to begin our days and live our lives!

I have lived those days so many times.

I dreaded waking up in the morning and going to work. Often, my body was wrapped in pain exhausted by the journey of the day before. I wondered, *Who cares about me? What is all of this for?* It felt as though my hopes and dreams had left me a long time ago, and I was merely existing. On the worst days, I felt like I was living among the ruins of my life, a dark landscape shaped by the bad choices I had made. I felt as though past decisions kept me from pursuing my dreams and that other people had prevented me from achieving what I wanted to achieve; it became really easy to blame others for the errors I made in my life. I had no hope to energize me, no promise of a prosperous life.

One day I began to really think about what my life was worth. *Why even bother to prepare for the next day?* I wondered. I began to pity myself. I told myself that if I was gone, no one would even miss me. I thought, *Everyone would be better off without me anyway. What is the use of me being here?*

Oh my goodness! What was I thinking? One day, the foolishness of my behavior hit me all at once. How selfish I was being by disregarding all the good in my life. I was also ignoring someone greater than all of my problems and circumstances—God. Even during my worst times, I was still telling people that God was awesome and that He could deliver them out of every situation. Well, what about me? Why couldn't I believe what I was preaching? I learned through the years that if we don't stand for what's right, we'll easily fall for what's wrong. I had to remember that Jesus is my answer, and that I must always look to Him.

I reminded myself that my undivided attention to God was my strength.

Reality is sometimes hard for us to face. However, when we face it with God's help, we feel a greater assurance that all will be well. Knowing that we can trust in Him gives us joy and a feeling that we can live well and be happy.

When we come to realize how great our God is, our lives can change. All we need is hope.

For surely I know the plans I have for you, says the Lord, plans for your welfare and not for harm, to give you a future with hope.

Jeremiah 29:11

MY DEVOTION

This is my devotion, I give You praise
Daily I will worship Your holy name
This is my devotion, my everything
Empty Your vessel, fill me again
Fill me again

So let Your word abide in me to be faithful
Every day, new mercies I see
Let Your sacrifice
forever remain in my heart for the world to see

—from the song written and composed by
  Pastor Darren Jenkins

||||||||||||||||||||||||||||||||||||||||||||||||||||||||||||||||||||||||||||||||||||||||||

"Faith is deliberate confidence in the character of God whose ways you may not understand at the time."

—Oswald Chambers

||||||||||||||||||||||||||||||||||||||||||||||||||||||||||||||||||||||||||||||||||||||||||

27

God IS the Author of Your Life

With God by my side, I know that my future is assured.
My life is in the hands of God. There is no need to
worry about where it will end.

GOD IS THE AUTHOR OF MY LIFE. It is He who will decide my beginning and my end and the shape of my days in between.

I can let go of the old story that I had written for myself, a story of mistakes and regrets. I once wrote a story of a life of heartache and despair for me. But I no longer have to live out those chapters of my life. I no longer have to walk alone or follow what other people instruct me to do. God is leading me to a new present and a new future. With God by my side, I am departing from a life of distractions and ceasing to focus on any object of failure. If I were to consider the hurt and the pain of my life all day every day, I would never be able to move on to accomplish the greater plan prepared for me. Instead, I must always focus on God's leading role in my life. He is the author of my faith.

I know that my future is assured, too. Many people are concerned about which way they will leave this world. That thought plagues some people every day. When I feel like this, I tell myself to have courage and know that my life is in the hands of God. There is no need to worry about where my life will end.

I must remember that God is the author of my life! I am free from the bondage of sin and death, and I am free to live a life of joy and of peace. While I am alive, God is transforming my life every day.

Having my eyes fixed on God leads me to a life of truth and prosperity. I have the assurance of knowing where my life has begun—and the certainty that God will guide the rest of it for all the days of my life.

There is a never-ending story in God.

. . . looking to Jesus the pioneer and perfecter of our faith, who for the sake of the joy that was set before him endured the cross, disregarding its shame, and has taken his seat at the right hand of the throne of God.

Hebrews 12:2

28

God IS By Your Side

Negative thoughts blind us and prevent us from seeing a door to opportunity. With God by my side, I learned that I could overcome negative feelings and feelings of rejection toward myself.

SOMETIMES WE ACT IN WAYS that are hurtful to ourselves.

I'm reminded of times when I met the needs of others without meeting my own needs. I didn't understand that although it was my obligation to help others, I first had to help myself. Instead of supporting myself so that I could function properly and effectively, I rejected myself and my own needs. This left me feeling used and empty. With nowhere to turn and my energy gone, I treated myself harshly rather than supportively. Soon, feelings of anxiety, helplessness, or abandonment washed over me. My emotional freedom—the freedom to feel good—was gone.

What we fail to recognize is that negative thoughts blind us and prevent us from seeing a door to opportunity. If we can stop our thoughts from becoming irrational and hurtful, we will find that life's challenges can be stepping-stones for growth.

We must recognize that God is great and He is powerful. Acknowledging this must be the first step. Then we must understand the importance of our relationship with God. With God by our sides, we can overcome anything. By placing your hand in the hand of God and allowing Him to lead you and guide you, you can overcome negative feelings.

With God by my side, I learned that negative feelings could not control me and that feelings of rejection could not conquer my spirit. Over time, refusing rejection helped me to elevate my self-esteem. I became stronger. Now, I can reach out to others and help them without feeling like I am abandoning myself.

For I, the Lord your God, hold your right hand; it is I who say to you, "Do not fear, I will help you."

Isaiah 41:13

29

God IS Your Voice

Even when we feel that a part of us has been weakened beyond repair, God is there to help us. When we fall silent because of shame or hurt, He will help us find our voice again.

THE BIBLE TELLS US OF GOD'S almighty power. There's no problem or issue that we have or that will come that God does not understand and cannot fix. No matter how many times we come up against what seems to be defeat and no matter what happens to us, God will help us.

Even when we feel that a part of us has been weakened beyond repair, God is there to help us. When we are weak, God is our strength. When we fall silent because of shame or hurt, He will help us find our voices again.

I know a woman who experienced terrible hardships when she was a little girl. She was only in the fourth grade when she was abused by an adult she trusted. She felt too ashamed and frightened to tell anyone. For years, she kept the secret of what she had experienced locked away inside herself. There it grew into dark feelings of shame, anger, and hurt. She could not heal.

As she became an adult, her secret continued to haunt her life. She could not trust anyone. She believed wholeheartedly that there could never be any good, in anyone. It was impossible for her to form relationships so she was utterly alone.

The Bible tells us in 2 Corinthians 12:9, ". . . So, I will boast all the more gladly of my weaknesses, so that the power of Christ may dwell in me." After this young woman turned to God for help, she found a source of strength that lifted her shame. She also found her voice again. Today that young lady spends her time mentoring young women all over her hometown, encouraging them to scream out loud about anything that seems harmful to them. With her help, young girls are not afraid to stand up for themselves and take control of their lives.

We can draw from the fountain of God's love at any time. He is there to guide our weary souls and help us find our voices so that we may live without fear, shame, or anger.

. . . but he said to me, "My grace is sufficient for you, for power is made perfect in weakness."

2 Corinthians 12:9

30

God IS Devotion

Just as in any relationship, it takes time to get to know God. Be devoted to God, and you will reap the fruits of emotional healing and spiritual growth.

FINDING OUR WAY THROUGH the commandments of God is not always easy. Yet, even though God's ways are not like ours, He is an awesome God and we must be devoted to Him.

I'm reminded of a young woman who was totally determined to live by the standards of God. She was dedicated to the work of the church and assisted in every aspect of ministry that she could. Any time the pastor needed help, she went. Whatever needed attending to, she was there.

However, deep down inside she felt a hole in her heart. It seemed as though every time she opened her heart to others, the emptiness grew wider. She could not understand why she felt this way. She began to ask God, "Why am I so lonely? I have done all that I was supposed to do, so why do I have this feeling?"

Then she developed alopecia, a disease that causes hair loss. She was only in her early 30s, and she could not understand why this was happening to her. She had turned her life around and committed her all to God. *How could the God I serve do this to me?* she wondered. This young woman, who was once vibrant and full of joy, felt full of hopelessness.

Now, my experience in my walk with God has taught me that although we will sometimes face battles that seem to overwhelm us, they will not overtake us.

As time went on, the young woman began to search the scriptures to find healing and restoration for her soul. She soon realized that God needed her devotion. Now, you might say, "Wasn't she already devoted to God?" The truth is that she hadn't given herself enough time with God. Sometimes we don't take the time we need to grow with God before, being as eager as we are, we begin working for Him. We can often find ourselves so busy with the challenges of ministry that we forget to stop and really learn what God is asking from us. *Just as in any relationship, it takes time to get to know God.* Time is required to build a connection and get to know each other. This young woman, enthused by her new relationship with God, forgot to stop and listen. After realizing the Lord was calling her to a deeper relationship with Him, my friend began to totally focus on God and His direction.

As my friend began to hear and understand what the Lord was saying, she realized God was calling her to grow in grace, rejoice in hope, and enjoy His glory. She became more tuned-in to God's will for her life. Her faith grew, and she began to reap the first fruits of emotional healing and spiritual growth. The Lord blessed her with some beauticians that were able to provide her with products to grow her hair back. Through much prayer, she learned that she was a living testimony of God's love, a witness for Him everywhere she went.

When God calls for your devotion, answer His call.

God is great.

Now to him who is able to keep you from falling, and to make you stand without blemish in the presence of his glory with rejoicing. . .

Jude 1:24

||||||||||||||||||||||||||||||||||||||||||||||||||||||||||||||||||||||||||||||||||||||||||||||

"Faith is to believe what you do not see; the reward of this faith is to see what you believe."

—Saint Augustine

||||||||||||||||||||||||||||||||||||||||||||||||||||||||||||||||||||||||||||||||||||||||||||||

31

God IS Real

The works of the Lord are bountiful. Let us appreciate
God's creations and be grateful for all He has given us.

THERE IS NOTHING MYTHICAL about God and all of
His power. The glory of God's work is all around us.

God reveals the work of His creation through what we
can see. The sky, the grass, the sun, and the very air that we
breathe say to us, *God is real.*

God has done the work to bring about all creation, includ-
ing ourselves. The ruler of our souls is the architect of our
very existence. When we see ourselves, we should remember
that we are made in the image of God. God in His matchless
power made us His very own creation.

God has provided for us. He causes fruit and vegetables to grow to nourish man. The wonders of this earth sustain life for us. How great are the provisions God has made for us.

God is the creator of the heavens and earth and of the work of man and woman. When we look at the man-made creations of this world, we still want to tribute that power to man. But man can't assume such greatness as his own, for it was through God that man is inspired to create, build, or change the landscape around us. When we look at anything man has made that is wondrous to us, let us remember that it is by God's strength that we are capable of doing anything.

The works of the Lord are bountiful. With Him, we are given a life of abundance, blessing, and wonder. The next time you are out in the world, take a moment to look all around you at God's creations and appreciate them.

Isn't the world we live in amazing? Let us be grateful for all God has given us.

And God said, "Let the earth bring forth living creatures of every kind: cattle and creeping things and wild animals of the earth of every kind." And it was so.

Genesis 1:24

32

God IS Joyful of His Creation

God makes the wonder of birth possible. It is an honor
to be part of creation.

HAVE YOU EVER SAT AND wondered about the
creations of man and woman, and how God makes
these achievements possible? For a moment, consider how
God has given women the ability to bring forth children.
This thought is so awesome and miraculous. As a mother, I
have myself felt this.

Often, I am in awe of how God has blessed me by allowing
me to be a mother. *God chose me and trusted me to carry a
child and give birth to a human being.* I feel so honored that
I am able to be part of creation. It is amazing that we can be
willing vessels used by God.

The anticipation of a helpless, innocent baby being born is so wonderful and brings such joy. Yes, we also experience fears; we may worry about how to be good parents or worry about the state of the world into which our child will be born. However, the joys that result when a baby arrives supercedes all anxieties and fears. When a baby is finally born, we are filled with relief. The moment we look at the face of a beautiful baby, we sigh or cry with joy. Oh wow, what beauty stands before you!

You look at this beautiful creation and you say to yourself, "This is God." *There's no way that man can do this all by himself.*

Bringing another being into the world is truly amazing. For when you look ahead and examine all of the possibilities of who this newborn baby could become, you are filled with awe. God looks at us, His creation, in the same way. But He has the infinite eye that sees no end: He sees the finished creation before it happens. God does not view us as man views us, for it is He that made us, not man. As the Bible states, "Know that the Lord is God. It is He that made us, and we are his; we are his people, and the sheep of his pasture" (Psalm 100:3).

God calls His creation good. Not one of us can escape that we were created by God.

Oh, God is so great!

God saw everything that he had made, and indeed, it was very good.

Genesis 1:31

33

God IS
Merciful

God shows us mercy and love on a daily basis, and
that is what He wants us to do for each other. We
have a lifetime obligation to show mercy—and most
of all, love—to those around us.

WHAT DO WE ATTRIBUTE to the word "mercy?" How,
when, and why have we needed it?

Mercy is unmerited favor. In other words, you and I didn't
have to do anything to deserve mercy. This mercy was granted
to us because of love.

To understand mercy borne of love, think for a moment of
someone dear to you. Have you ever loved someone so much
that your heart bleeds for them no matter what misdeed he
or she's done? Despite their wrongdoings, you have a burning
desire to forgive them.

I am thinking of a young woman whom I loved very much (and still do). But, somehow, I could never fully convince her that the love I offered was truly genuine. Because of hurt and betrayal in her life, she did not know how to receive love and friendship from others. In fact, she acted out her pain by hurting those around her. Often, I became the recipient of her rejection.

The Bible tells us to do unto others as you would have them to do unto you. Consider this: If we neglect to offer the true love within us to someone else—love that can heal and help—then we will continue to foster the "eye for an eye, tooth for a tooth" concept. We will be infected with a generation of mean, hurtful people, and our world will contribute evil for evil.

It is God's mercy that has been given to us that will save us from this fate. Remember that nothing good has been done on our own; but for the grace of God are we granted yet another day. And this day, like every day, is an opportunity to make a difference in the lives of others.

I still can't comprehend what keeps this young lady from experiencing the fullness and joy of her life. But I have a lifetime obligation to show her mercy and, most of all, love. That's what God does for us on a daily basis, and that is what He wants us to do for each other.

Blessed be the God and Father of our Lord Jesus Christ! By his great mercy he has given us a new birth into a living hope. . .

1 Peter 1:3

34

God IS Just

Sometimes it may not feel like God sees or knows the injustice that has been dealt to us. But He really does. The next time we make our supplications known to God, seek the wisdom He offers you. Then, you will know justice.

A LL OF US HAVE EXPERIENCED injustice in one way or another. But how often do we consider what injustice really is? Do we understand its full meaning?

I am reminded of the story in the Bible from the book of Kings. In this story, two women both gave birth to baby boys. But one woman's child had died. The mother of the deceased was distraught, angry, and jealous, all at the same time. She purposed in her heart a deceitful scheme to obtain a child.

She set out to steal another woman's child and claim him as hers. Then, she would falsely state that this woman had taken *her* child because she had lost her own baby. *What extremes the enemy would go to in order to prevail.*

Of course, this matter caused a huge spectacle. Who would decide which woman was telling the truth and which was telling a lie?

King Solomon reigned as king at that time. The Lord was pleased with Solomon. When the Lord told Solomon to make a request, any request, known unto God and He would grant it, instead of asking for riches, Solomon asked for wisdom and understanding so that he could better lead God's people. Not only did God grant Solomon his request, but He also blessed him with riches and glory.

The incident between the two women was the first of many matters concerning his people that the king would have to deal with. Using the wisdom that God had given to him, King Solomon suggested that the baby be cut in half and shared between the two women. The mother of the child cried out in horror at the possibility that her baby would be harmed. She suggested the child be given to the other woman. The other woman suggested that the child be killed so neither would have the child.

Upon seeing the compassion of the first woman for the life of the child, King Solomon wisely determined that she was the mother. Solomon's people looked on in awe as they witnessed the wisdom of God that had been attained in him. Justice was served by God through His yielded vessel, King Solomon. King Solomon knew what to ask for—wisdom—in order to be a successful king of Israel.

We serve a God who favors truth. Sometimes it may not feel like God sees or knows about the injustice that has been dealt to us. But He really does. Like Solomon, we must have a balanced and real relationship with God to receive all of His benefits. The next time you make your supplications known to God, seek the wisdom He offers you. Then God will bring about justice for you.

The Rock,his work is perfect, and all his ways are just. A faithful God, without deceit, just and upright is he. . .

Deuteronomy 32:4

||||||||||||||||||||||||||||||||||||||||||||||||||||||||||||||||||||||||||||||||||||||||||||

"Let us raise a standard to which the wise and the honest can repair. The event is in the hand of God."

—George Washington

||||||||||||||||||||||||||||||||||||||||||||||||||||||||||||||||||||||||||||||||||||||||||||

35

God IS Your Future

God redeems our lives from a past of destruction.
He then showers us with love and kindness. He
renews us.

A S WE GO THROUGH LIFE, HANDLING the guilt of our
past can be one of the most challenging undertakings.
Sometimes we overwhelm ourselves with constant reminders
of the actual events that occurred. This can be excruciating. Even worse, the hurt and pain caused can stagnate our
progression. For those of us judged by others for our past
mistakes, the taunting remarks hurled at you can cause even
greater setbacks.

With so many trials and twists and turns, it can be hard
to see a future for yourself and life can be disheartening.

Anyone who has been convicted of a crime knows far too well that filling out a job application can be one of the most frightening experiences.

I'm reminded of a young woman's story. She was convicted and jailed for homicide. Although she committed the crime to save her life and her child's life, she was sentenced to 20 years without parole. Although she was set free on technicalities after 5 years, her life was nevertheless in ruins. The crime remained on her record. Unfortunately, in the eyes of society, once you have been convicted, it's a done deal. Your life is pretty much over.

In the case of this young woman, you have to wonder who would give her a fighting chance to right the wrong in her life.

God has a way that is mighty sweet. While spending time in the correctional facility, Christians had come to visit the young woman. They counseled her and helped her. At first she was not receptive. She did not feel that what they were saying could help her; after all, it seemed her life had pretty much been determined. But as time went on, she began to listen. She thought about a second chance for herself. She prayed and asked for forgiveness. She also forgave herself.

After being set free, she found she had nowhere to turn. Lost time with her loved ones was detrimental to her relationships. Trust was lost, and friends became few. She felt alone in such a huge world. Trying to keep her negative thoughts at bay was so challenging all by herself.

Soon she sought God for direction. She joined a church. Things were difficult at first. But she kept the faith. Through perseverance, she broke through the barriers of defeat, mistakes, hurt, and pain. She was able to get a job, and as time progressed she learned how to trust herself again and form a healthy relationship with a man. They soon married, and the church members helped her get her daughter back. She maintained her goal in life and conquered her past and her former doubts. Today she is a lawyer and enjoys her life as a wife and mother.

Imagine that: a new life after a life of heartache and fear; a new path to peace and prosperity. *God's redeeming power is so awesome.* When we turn to Him, He redeems our lives from a past of destruction. He then showers us with love and kindness. He renews us.

God can erase your past and restore your future for greatness.

. . . who forgives all your iniquity, who heals all your diseases, who redeems your life from the Pit, who crowns you with steadfast love and mercy, who satisfies you with good as long as you live so that your youth is renewed like the eagle's.

Psalm 103:3-4

||||||||||||||||||||||||||||||||||||||||||||||||||||||||||||||||||||||||||||||||||||||||||||||||||||||||||

"God moves in a mysterious way
His wonders to perform;
He plants his footsteps in the sea,
and rides upon the storm."

—William Cowper,
"Light Shining Out of Darkness"

||||||||||||||||||||||||||||||||||||||||||||||||||||||||||||||||||||||||||||||||||||||||||||||||||||||||||

36

God IS Unity

Marriage ordained by God is a sacred union, a union
never to be broken. Couples should take heart and be
encouraged that through them, God is able to touch
more lives than they even realize.

MATHEMATICS WAS ALWAYS a subject that I struggled
with in school. After a while, I decided that knowing
the basics was enough for me. If I could put two and two
together and understand subtraction well enough to know
when someone was taking money from me, I was good.

Then one day I learned about the Lord's mathematics.
When marriage is ordained by God, two people are no longer
two, but one. Over the years, my understanding of this has
become deeper and stronger, better and greater.

My husband, Darren Jenkins Sr., and I have been married for 21 years. Marrying at a young age had its challenges from the beginning. Throughout the marriage we have experienced some amazing triumphs and some failures. We have plunged into depths of sorrow, experienced betrayal, and known loss that we didn't think was possible. We have had some dreams realized and some dreams shattered.

Although my husband and I don't know everything and, for many years, we didn't know what our life would be like, one thing we never wanted to do was forsake what God had given to us. *How could we tamper with an anointed and blessed match ordained by God?* We loved the Lord, and we knew and understood the concept of love and unity.

Laboring for the Lord is a lifetime commitment. The word of God says that whoever puts their hand to the plow and looks back is not worthy for the work. I have learned that there are many demands, but the joys far outweigh the difficulties. I have also learned that everything I thought about marriage before I was wed is actually null and void! To make marriage work, I had to let go of all of my ideas and views about marriage and totally depend on God to see me through. I have truly relied on the biblical teachings concerning how I should be as a wife. Understanding these teachings helps me to respect my role and understand God's purpose for me.

When God has joined two people together, this is not a mistake. In our years together as a couple, God has taken our pain and loss and turned these ashes into something beautiful. We know more today about what it means to walk with faith than ever before. Without God, we can do nothing;

together, we are united to serve. Marriage is the ministry of God and the illuminated love of Christ.

God is so awesome in His demonstration of love through marriage. Today I can look back on 21 years of marriage and see that we have reached amazing heights of which we would not have dared to dream. Darren and I are going strong in our marriage and these are the best years of our lives. I wouldn't trade my marriage for anything else, and I am so glad to have been able to totally trust in God throughout our marriage. Being married is a great joy, a great responsibility, and a great blessing.

Marriage ordained by God is a sacred union, a union never to be broken. I would advise every married couple to take heart and be encouraged that through you, God is able to touch more lives than you even realize. The Lord is using your love for good in more ways than you know. Remember too that God is your strength and power, and it is He that makes your way perfect.

Be glad in the Lord and rejoice. May each happy moment fill your days with beautiful reflections, continued success, and the continual joy you both deserve.

So they are no longer two, but one flesh. Therefore what God has joined together, let no one separate.

Matthew 19:6

||||||||||||||||||||||||||||||||||||||||||||||||||||||||||||||||||||||||||||||||||||||||||||||||||

"The soul can split the sky in two,
and let the face of God shine through."

—Edna St. Vincent Millay, "Renascence"

||||||||||||||||||||||||||||||||||||||||||||||||||||||||||||||||||||||||||||||||||||||||||||||||||

37

God IS
Freedom

There is no need to walk in fear when God is the author of our lives. Walk in the liberty of God. Pursue your destiny in Him by acknowledging your freedom.

W HAT IS FREEDOM? We often think of freedom as the ability to live as we like without restrictions, to use liberty and our own free will to make decisions.

When we feel like we are prevented from being free, it is often because our own fears keep us in bondage. We often fail to realize this, and instead place blame on others.

This bondage begins in the mind. Scattered thoughts of negative outcomes take over our thoughts. Fear soon dominates. Fear is one of the greatest obstacles to one's progress. When one is living in fear, challenges become greater, responsibility seems enormous, and success is impossible.

I am reminded of an individual who let fear stop him. This person had the opportunity to enjoy a fulfilling career by using his skills as a fashion designer. He was wonderfully creative, produced great sketches, was an excellent worker, and could speedily execute a job when needed.

However, when someone proposed a major deal to him— one that was sure to lead to great profit and fortune—fear took a grip on him and would not let go. He walked away. Even worse, he resolved to never show his work to anyone again. When I later asked why he never pursued the opportunity to let the greatness he possessed reach the world, he simply answered that it was because of the "fear of being free."

Because this young man was comfortable with a certain lifestyle, the thought of moving forward from that place was too much for him. The thought of having responsibility greater than what he knew overtook him. The sense of doubt in his mind grew into fear that prevented him from moving forward.

Freedom and fear don't mix. Fear is what keeps us from true freedom. Allow me to remind you: *There is no need to walk in fear when God is the author of our lives. God has set us free.*

We have to learn how to refuse fear immediately. Don't let wayward emotions that contradict God's word rule your decisions and stop you from being free. Instead, walk in the liberty of God. Pursue your destiny in Him by acknowledging your freedom.

For freedom Christ has set us free. Stand firm, therefore, and do not submit again to a yoke of slavery.

Galatians 5:1

38

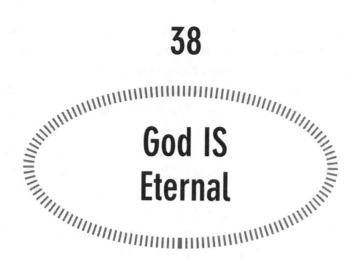

God IS Eternal

God is everlasting to everlasting. He is an eternal source of never-ceasing love.

WOULDN'T IT BE WONDERFUL TO KNOW that the love we have for another is eternal and that the relationships we build could last forever?

When we come to love one another, it is hard to think that we will one day never see each other in the physical realm. Although it sometimes feels like it will never end, our time here with one another is short. We would love to stay in a place where friends and family would never leave us. Losing someone is hard. We cannot have insurance to cover those kinds of losses. It can be difficult to face. If we lose someone, we sometimes dream that this person will come back to us.

Unfortunately, this can't be. One day we will all come to the end, whether it's due to a relationship gone wrong, someone moving away, or the death of someone dear to us.

God is everlasting to everlasting; compared to God, man's life is but grass that withers. I have experienced some losses in my life that made me feel as if I could not go on. In the past 6 months, I have dealt with the loss of two fathers. And yet, looking back, I would say that I have never experienced love—through God—like this before. My God is eternal, a source of never-ceasing love that extends beyond my own imagination. He will never leave me or forsake me. His love reaches to places I thought were untouchable.

Even in hard times, the thought that God is so great in His power and that His love is infinite and eternal gives me peace and hope.

Lord, you have been our dwelling-place in all generations. Before the mountains were brought forth, or ever you had formed the earth and the world, from everlasting to everlasting you are God.

Psalm 90:1–2

39

God IS a Healer

After God extends His hand and we accept His healing, we often relive our past mistakes over and over again. We reopen the wound. Whenever God moves to heal us, let us trust Him completely, embrace his long-term plan for our lives, and move forward.

DO YOU REMEMBER FALLING and scraping your knee as a child? Oh, the excruciating pain of the raw wound! Sometimes the pain was minor compared to the agony of looking at the wound itself: It was shocking to see the skin peeled away and to see it bleed. If we hadn't already started yelling for help, the sight of the wound certainly made us scream and cry.

At the sound of our cries, our moms would come to our rescue. It was such a relief to have her there! Sometimes we even screamed a little louder after she had arrived just to get more affection from her. She doctored the wound, and we felt better right away. Let's not forget the treats we got after the injury—the extra whipped cream on our ice cream cone or two lollipops instead of one. All this made us feel awfully special.

But then the attention would fade away.

To get it back, maybe we peeled back the bandage and picked the wound until it bled. All this pain, just to receive that special attention all over again. Unfortunately, the additional attention was not as good as it was the first time. Usually, our moms knew what we had been up to. We realized that we should have just left well enough alone.

That's how some of us live our lives today. After God extends His hand and we accept His healing, we often relive our past mistakes over and over again. We reopen the wound. We reminisce about all the bad that has happened and have a "pity party." Instead of acknowledging how we have been healed, we bring up past hurts and cause ourselves pain.

Why? Why are we more attracted to the drama of pain than healing? Is this because it seems "too good to be true" that God could really, truly heal us from something? Does part of us think we know better than He knows?

Let us stop living a "pity party." We should not find reason to fault God just so we can feel badly for ourselves. Put your faith in God and truly trust that He has your life in control, He loves you, and He is concerned about your life.

Whenever God moves to heal us, let us trust Him completely. After we are healed, let us continue to embrace his long-term plans for our lives and move forward instead of looking back.

God can heal us completely and make us whole again, if we allow him to.

... endurance produces character, and character produces hope, and hope does not disappoint us, because God's love has been poured into our hearts through the Holy Spirit that has been given to us.

Romans 5:4–5

I COME CLOSER

I come closer, Lord, to know just who You are
I draw nearer, Lord, I come after Your heart

I incline my ears to hear You speak
I open eye to see Your ways
My heart surrenders to Your will
To follow You is my desire

—from the song written and composed by
Pastor Darren Jenkins

‖‖‖

"With God in charge, I believe everything will work out for the best in the end. So what is there to worry about?"

—Henry Ford

‖‖‖

40

God IS Your Solution

Our own solutions often only provide short-term answers, but looking to God provides a cure that will keep us strong for all the days of our lives.

I REMEMBER A TIME IN MY LIFE when I did not feel well. Although I knew something was not right, I could not quite determine the cause. Pain overtook my body and my spirit. I went to the doctor but the medication did not help me. I had no energy. I could not move forward. Others tried to offer resolution. Many gave me advice.

But only answers from God should be accepted.

Some days we forget about God and the difference His presence has made in our lives. It could be that we ourselves or our family or friends are struggling with physical, emotional, or spiritual problems that just don't seem to get any better. We may even think to ourselves that those who trust solely in God are destined to lose the fight. Although we have experienced many daunting challenges that God has brought us through, we forget how God has made it possible. We somehow negate the help that our God offers us. We know what the Bible says, but we may still question God's power.

But this assessment is only the result of a faulty mindset. At times like these, we must remind ourselves of the greatest, most powerful truth of all: We serve an understanding, mighty God, and He is always here to help us.

Our own solutions often only provide short-term answers, but looking to God provides a cure that will keep us strong for all the days of our lives. When times get tough, we must have a discerning heart and be careful not to accept quick fixes. We really don't need a false diagnosis that harms us more than it helps us or an easy answer that works like "suppressive medicine"—something that suppresses the problem rather than clearing it up for good.

There's no problem or issue that we have now or will have in the future that God cannot handle. No matter how many times we feel defeated, God is here to help us.

Cultivate a great appreciation of God's power in you. Rely chiefly on God to help you as you go through life.

Trust God in His unwavering and infinite understanding.

Great is our Lord, and abundant in power; his understanding is beyond measure.

Psalm 147:5

41

God IS Comfort

No matter from where our crying stems, as we cry unto the Lord, He is faithful to us. He will hear us and He will answer.

A T ONE POINT OR ANOTHER, we have all cried so that someone would hear us. As children, we cried like this until a comforting parent or loved one came to soothe us.

Once we are grown, although we may not always shed tears, we are all crying out in some way. Some cry out in passion, anger, hurt, or rejection. Of course, we also cry out in delight, happiness, and joy. It's hard to believe that a single word, "cry," can be attributed to so many different ways of feeling and expressing ourselves.

As adults, who hears our cries? That is the question.

I remember standing in the shower one day. I visualized the flow of the water as rain, and as I stood still and allowed the water to fall around me, I seized the opportunity to cry. Although many things were on my mind, this weeping was not for any specific event or person. It was an expression of many feelings. Crying was a release of tension for me. I started out crying very quietly, but within minutes, the intensity of the crying increased. I cried louder and louder. I found myself just not wanting to stop. Even screams came.

At first, I wanted someone to hear me. But then I started to calm down. As I stood there, I began to listen to the drops of water hit the tub. I tried to reverse my thinking and, instead of seeing agony and stress, I started to visualize the drops of water as overflowing blessings. As I looked up at the drops of water hitting my face, my sorrowful crying became a cry of exultation. I saw God lift my burden of lamenting and turn that moment into a time for rejoicing. I felt God was assuring me that He heard me. As the Bible tells us in Psalm 30:5, "For his anger is but for a moment; his favour is for a lifetime. Weeping may linger for the night, but joy comes with the morning."

Sometimes we see our suffering as an indication of being victimized with no hope. *Let us not forget that God is our hope in every situation.*

The troubles we face are not there to cause grief or disappoint us. In the end, *all things work out for the better.* As the Bible reminds us in the book of Romans 8:28, "We know that all things work together for good for those who love God, who are called according to his purpose."

Let me be clear that there is nothing wrong with crying. In fact, it can be helpful. But just remember that no matter from where our crying stems, as we cry unto the Lord, He is faithful to us. He will hear us and He will answer.

Go ahead and cry and allow your healing to take place. God awaits our cry unto Him. We are His children, and He is eager to answer us when we call.

May those who sow in tears reap with shouts of joy.

Psalm 126:5

III

"All are but parts of one stupendous whole,
Whose body Nature is, and God the soul."

—Alexander Pope, "An Essay on Man"

IIIIIIIIIIIIIIIIIIIIIIIIIIIIIIIIIIIIIIIIIIIIIIIIIIIIIIIIIIIIIIIIIIIIIIIIIIIIIIIIIIIIIIIIIIIIIII

42

God IS
Caring

We should always turn to God for help. God is always
there to listen, in good times and bad.

W HEN SOMETHING GOOD happens in our lives, we are
usually eager to share the exciting news. We expect
a joyful response from friends and family. Often, we share a
celebration together.

Yet when we find ourselves in trouble, it is harder for us to
share this with others. We don't want to admit to another that
we are struggling. *Pride is a real tough thing.* Sometimes the
last thing we want to do is tell someone about our problems. I
can identify with those who have been troubled by mistakes,
bad luck, or hardships, but who don't reach out to someone
for help.

This can be a big mistake. By refusing to get the help we need, we deny ourselves a chance at living a full life.

Certainly, we have all had both good and bad experiences. If we were to really look closely at all the events in our lives, most of us would say the good outweighs the bad. Yet most of us make the mistake of failing to see the big picture of our lives. Instead, we focus on the negative. We let the bad times that have happened to us steer our decisions and decide our future. Negative experiences make us afraid. They keep us from enjoying life. With fear in our hearts we will be hesitant to try new things. Reluctance can keep us from experiencing true friendships, lasting relationships, and real love. Essentially, we allow negative experiences from our past to destroy any chance at a bright, wonderful future. We throw away what we never even knew we could have!

All this can be avoided if we allow ourselves to ask for help. When help is offered and a hand is extended to us, we are to receive the hand given.

The Bible declares in James 4:2, ". . . You do not have, because you do not ask." *We should always ask God for help.* Our relationship with Him is not one-sided: God is always there to listen, in good times and bad. The most gracious and everlasting God in we serve will always take the time to hear us.

God looks for us to turn toward Him. He's waiting to hear us. The Lord God is the source of our joy and desires joyfulness for us, His people. *He is always willing to help.*

And this is the boldness we have in him, that if we ask anything according to his will, he hears us.

1 John 5:14

43

God IS Constant

Despite so much change in our lives, God is always constant.

WHEN WE RISE EACH DAY, we experience something different. No day is exactly the same as the day before it. be different.

With every season that passes, we feel how the temperature changes and we witness how the leaves on the trees change color. The natural environment around us is always changing.

We ourselves are also constantly changing in both our bodies and minds. In our minds, our thoughts, concerns, and ideas sway back and forth. We are constantly reevaluating our priorities based on our experiences. As the years go by, what we have endured may even cause us to reevaluate the values instilled in us. We may find that the issues we used to care about don't mean as much or do not carry the same weight as they used to. As we age, our physical appearance also changes.

It can be difficult to accept the true value of change and, more important, to appreciate it. We become accustomed to what's familiar in our lives—and even if what's familiar to us brings us heartache and pain, we feel more comfortable with it because we are used to it. *We like to know what's coming.* When we don't know what's coming our way, we may tend to shy away from the new possibilities that change can present to us.

But we can also embrace change as an opportunity. We can look forward to the future and enjoy the anticipation of something new. When I awake each day, I try to be excited about the possibilities that await me, instead of getting anxious.

In everything around us, we witness the truth: Nothing ever really stays the same. However, I have found that despite so much change in our lives, God is always constant.

God never changes. We can turn to this truth for comfort when life seems uncertain, and knowing this can help us enjoy all that life has to offer.

Cast all your anxiety on him, because he cares for you.

1 Peter 5:7

44

God IS Your Example

God never wants us to give up on bringing change to people's lives. Let us carefully learn the ways of the great God and adhere to His ways so that we can lead as examples.

WE SOMETIMES FAIL TO REALIZE that we carry a lot of unnecessary baggage with us that weighs us down and shifts our focus away from what is valuable in life. This baggage can be anything, from past mistakes to bad habits. Following a leader can help to clarify our focus.

People can be living, vivid examples of how to lead a loving and just life. We can be valuable examples to each other.

At some point in our lives, almost all of us have looked to another as an example of how we should live. To follow an individual as an example requires time, effort, and commitment.

As a flock follows its shepherd willfully, so should we follow Christ as our example. Christ provides an example of good leadership, as well as an example of how to love. *When we exemplify these things, we prove that God is our example.*

A good leader is one who works with people and guides with love and patience. Genuine leaders rarely work alone. Christ showed excellent leadership skills. Although He could was capable of doing the work alone, He called for disciples and taught them how to follow so that they could one day lead.

The love of God is the greatest example of how to love others. Christ loves everyone. We all belong to Him equally. We can never be divided by the diversity of our cultures or colors of our skin. Christ took the time to lead and teach each individual He met. In this same way, we must never be biased toward others.

Many individuals working together can multiply the results of their efforts. Accomplishment is measured not by individual achievements, but by the success of the group. The good leader builds lasting bridges of unity. A diverse group of people, each inspired by a great example and each committed to one common cause, can bring about great change.

Following our Lord as an example requires sacrifice on our part. There is no middle ground. The Bible says in Luke 14:33, "So therefore, none of you can become my disciple if you do not give up all your possessions." In this passage, the Lord was letting his disciples know that they could not bring their attachments to worldly things with them on their journey with Him. You must be willing to forsake the riches, the fame, and all the glory of men, or else you are not ready to follow. There will often be opposition when we begin to do a good work for a great cause. This is unfortunate, but it is a trial we must all face. However, we can accomplish so much with great determination.

I am moved with enthusiasm when I see the methods of our Lord being utilized to bring forth love, unity, and prosperity.

God wants us to never give up on bringing change to people's lives. Let us carefully learn the ways of the great God and adhere to His ways so that we can lead as examples. We can do this by earnestly seeking to be like Christ. Let us exemplify love, trust, patience, hospitality, purity, holiness, humility, willingness, unselfishness, impartiality—the list can go on—in all that we do.

For to this you have been called, because Christ also suffered for you, leaving you an example, so that you should follow in his steps.

1 Peter 2:21

|||||||||||||||||||||||||||||||||||||||||||||||||||||||||||||||||||||||||||||||||||||||

"Let God's promises shine on your problems."

—Corrie ten Boom

|||||||||||||||||||||||||||||||||||||||||||||||||||||||||||||||||||||||||||||||||||||||

45

God IS
Peace

Wo can crcatc a calm place for ourselves at any time.
The doorway to peace lies within us, if we only look
to God.

W**HEN I THINK OF PEACE,** I think of still waters,
of calmness and a quiet place. I imagine a place of
solitude that brings comfort. And I think of God.

The greatest peace lies with God. The peace offered by a
quiet place is temporary; the time will come when we have to
leave that place. But the peace of God doesn't come and go.
It is everlasting. As the Bible tells us in Isaiah 9:6, our Lord
is "Wonderful Counsellor, Mighty God, Everlasting Father,
Prince of Peace."

We all need some peace in our lives. Even if we are not wrestling with huge problems, really busy days can be enough to overwhelm us. We may even want to scream out loud for a chance to enjoy some peace and quiet! Everyday problems have become more of a challenge lately for many of us, and not just because our lives are so busy. Simply covering the cost of living—groceries, bills, and other essentials—has become a trial. We may have lost a job ourselves, or we may have assumed responsibilities for someone else to help to ease his or her burden. Tasks that were once simple, like paying bills or buying food and clothing, can become a source of anxiety.

At times like these, we can turn to God for a moment of respite. We can create a calm place for ourselves at any time. The doorway to peace lies within us, if we only look to God. To do this, displace thoughts that are not pure and safe. Let the peace of God wash over you. As the Bible tells us in 1 Peter 3:11, "let them turn away from evil and do good; let them seek peace and pursue it."

In the middle of a busy day, when we are surrounded by others, we can turn to God for a break. Even if we feel overwhelmed with worry, we can rely on God.

It is wonderful to know that no matter the issues that life brings, I serve a God that is a source of peace. Even when difficult circumstances surround me and unresolved problems linger, God is always there. No matter what I am dealing with, there is always a way of escape: I can seek shelter and calm in God's loving care.

While the turmoil of the world swirls around us, we can have peace in the midst of it all, if we only look to God.

May the Lord give strength to his people! May the Lord bless his people with peace!

Psalm 29:11

‖‖

"Faith is the strength by which a shattered world shall emerge into the light."

—Helen Keller

‖‖

46

God IS True

Sometimes in our eagerness for truth, we can be led
astray. God's way is the way of truth. We cannot in
any way base our worship on our imagination.

THE WORD "TRUTH" DENOTES something stable,
reliable, and trustworthy. "Truth" means "established
fact."

Sometimes we try to take shortcuts or twist the truth to
an outcome we desire. Because we may be eager to retrieve a
reward or achieve some end result, we may convince ourselves
that something is true or trustworthy when, deep down, we
know it is not.

I can recall a time when my family and I experienced a
minor car accident. There were no injuries to my family, but

the car was damaged. After the accident, my husband and I were parked in the grocery store parking lot when a young man approached us. He said he had experience working on automobiles, and he told us that he could repair our car just like a professional but at a lower cost. We thought to ourselves, *Wow, that would be great!* We were eager to save some money. Even though we didn't know the young man, we decided to have him do the job for us.

As he worked on our car, we began to notice a change. . . for the worse. We told the young man that it did not look good, but he pleaded with us to be patient. He told us he wasn't done and that it would look a lot better once he finished. When the job was finally complete, we were amazed. We couldn't believe how awful the finished work was! We wished we would have just gone to the professionals. The young man who worked on our car had promised a solution. But what he had really offered was a quick fix that got us nowhere. The truth of the matter was that he really could not fix the damage completely. Although it would have cost slightly more to go to the professionals, the job would have been done right, and the outcome would have been assured. This is what we should have done.

It is the same with our relationship to our Lord. The commands of God are true and sure, but we sometimes ignore them, twist them around, or try to find a shortcut by ourselves. God's way is the way of truth. If we call ourselves people of God, then we should walk in a way that exemplifies our worship. We cannot in any way base our worship on our imagination or our own "best guess." We must be in sync, in harmony, with God. We must not be derailed by the misleading actions of others.

Let us represent truth and flee from evil presented as a lie. Everything that emanates from God is pure and true. No matter how we try to change the word of God, it is infallible.

For the word of the Lord is upright, and all his work is done in faithfulness.

Psalm 33:4

||||||||||||||||||||||||||||||||||||||||||||||||||||||||||||||||||||||||||||||||||||||||||||||||

"... though our feelings come and go, His love for us does not."

—C.S. Lewis

||||||||||||||||||||||||||||||||||||||||||||||||||||||||||||||||||||||||||||||||||||||||||||||||

47

God IS Nourishment

Let us be nourished daily by the word of God, for He is our source of strength.

WE KNOW THAT OUR BODIES will not be well unless we feed ourselves properly. Without nourishment, we begin to weaken. Our bodies must be maintained with a steady supply of essentials like iron, vitamins, and other nutrients. Even the mind has to be stimulated by daily reading and learning. If any one of these requirements is not met, eventually the body will break down. I know this well because, as the parents of three children, my husband and I choose the diet for the family. I always work to make sure my children eat healthy, nourishing food.

The body will die of malnourishment if it is not fed; so it is with our need for spiritual nourishment. In order to gain this spiritual strength and resist weakness, we must be nourished by the word of God. As the Bible states in 1 Timothy 4:6, "If you put these instructions before the brothers and sisters, you will be a good servant of Christ Jesus, nourished on the words of the faith and of the sound teaching that you have followed."

This lesson reminds me of the story of a young man. He was committed to God and was ordained as a pastor. After receiving a call to be the pastor of a church in his community, he committed himself to helping and serving the people in every way possible. He made house calls and visited the sick in the hospital. He accepted invitations for speaking engagements to preach the word of the Lord. He said yes to every call that came in. Soon it became quite evident that his workload was overwhelming and that his schedule was overbooked. He lacked the time he needed to read and study the word of God. Even after recognizing this, he still proceeded in the same fashion. His prayer life was hindered because he spent more time running to the rescue of others. Eventually, he burnt himself out, and he was no good to himself or anyone else.

We must be plugged in to the source. In other words, we must fill up with God's word in the Bible to be able to absorb the everyday cares of this life. For nourishment to be sustaining, it must be consistent and it must be maintained. Wearing ourselves out only defeats the purpose. It hinders our ability to do God's work. Our spiritual maintenance is of extreme importance.

God would never leave His people without nourishment. God does not expect His people to be superheroes. He does not expect us to do anything and everything on our own. However, we must spend time with the Father to receive the fullness of what He has to offer. He wants us to sit at His feet and seek direction from Him.

Always know that God is sympathetic to the needs of His people. It is up to us to go and seek Him for our needs.

Everyone knows that a vehicle cannot run properly without maintenance. A car can't even start without gasoline. Let's fill up so we can sustain ourselves on this walk. We are the vehicles God uses to deliver His message, and we must nourish ourselves to do so.

Let us be nourished daily by the word of God, for He is our source of strength.

. . . One does not live by bread alone, but by every word that comes from the mouth of God.

Matthew 4:4

||||||||||||||||||||||||||||||||||||||||||||||||||||||||||||||||||||||||||||||||||||||||

"When you say a situation or a person is hopeless, you are slamming the door in the face of God."

—Charles L. Allen

||||||||||||||||||||||||||||||||||||||||||||||||||||||||||||||||||||||||||||||||||||||||

48

God IS Family

Our extended family of friends, neighbors, co-workers, and acquaintances makes up part of our extended family. We are a unified people responsible for sharing love, as exemplified by God, with each other.

IN THE MODERN ERA, THERE are many ways to define "family." Whether we realize it or not, many of us are part of many different kinds of families. Your neighbors, relatives, friends, and co-workers are all members of an extended family. Although we can sometimes overlook them, relationships like these are blessings. In my life, I have found it a privilege to have an extended family outside of my home.

Yet it can be hard to invite people into our homes, let alone our lives. When I was growing up, my parents struggled with this. When I was a child, our parents did not allow my siblings and I to visit our neighbors' houses. In fact, we were not even permitted to have friends come over. I did not understand this at first, but as the years went by, I finally realized that my parents were just doing their best to protect their children. Coming from this background, it took me some time to learn the value of relationships with those outside my family.

My first lesson came when I visited my husband's family. His parents were *always* surrounded by people! They never turned anyone away. So many were welcomed into their home, and no matter how many visitors there were, there was always love and laughter to spare. I witnessed them welcome people from all walks of life into their lives. I was truly amazed. Today, I often tell others how awesome I think the love is that my husband extends to others. I am certain that this love originates from his upbringing in such a warm and welcoming home.

The Bible tells us in Hebrews 13:2, "Do not neglect to show hospitality to strangers, for by doing that some have entertained angels without knowing it." We can cultivate meaningful relationships, as God would like us to do. Any moment can be an opportunity. Think of the last time you ran into someone you had not seen in a long time. This can be a chance to make an old connection new again. You may be surprised to find out that you have a lot more in common that you thought—or you may even realize that you live two doors down from each other or work in the same neighborhood! It is a "small world." Don't let your friendships begin and end with, "Wow, it's been a while!" Keep those connections strong.

Everything has a divine purpose and order. The next time we see our brother or sister in trouble or realize we have distanced ourselves from another by a long quarrel, let us be reminded that God, the Father of us all, is watching us to see how we treat one another. We don't get to choose who enters into our lives, but we can choose how to welcome them. Our extended family of friends, neighbors, co-workers, and acquaintances is wonderfully diverse. No matter what our culture or background, we must realize we are all family. We are one unit designed to fulfill one purpose, one cause: *We are a unified people responsible for sharing love, as exemplified by God, with each other.*

We are all family because God is the head of us all.

For this reason I bow my knees before the Father, from whom every family in heaven and on earth takes its name.

Ephesians 3:14–15

||||||||||||||||||||||||||||||||||||||||||||||||||||||||||||||||||||||||||||||||||||||||||||||||

"Have faith in God; God has faith in you."

—Edwin Louis Cole

||||||||||||||||||||||||||||||||||||||||||||||||||||||||||||||||||||||||||||||||||||||||||||||||

49

God IS Prosperity

God has given us gifts that ensure we can obtain all
we need, and far more. One of the reasons that God
wants us to be successful is so we can share with
others.

A S WE FOLLOW GOD'S COMMANDMENTS during our
walk here on earth, we can sometimes feel limited in
our abilities. We may start to suspect personal growth or
prosperity is not a possibility for us. *That is not true.*

God desires for us to be prosperous and to achieve great
things in our lives. God wants us to reach for nothing less
than greatness. The Bible says in Deuteronomy 30:9, "... and
the Lord your God will make you abundantly prosperous in

all your undertakings. . ." The Lord wants for us to live rich, full lives.

What God *doesn't* want us to do is achieve greatness and forget that He made it possible. He wants us to remember who allowed us to prosper. It can be so easy to forget that God is the secret behind our success! He also wants us to share our good fortune with others.

When I think about people who have worked at the same place for a long time, I often wonder if, over the years, they began to put their trust in their jobs—instead of putting their trust in God. This is a mistake that we often make. We forget that it is God who provides for us. Unlike employment, which can be here today and then gone tomorrow, God is always with us. Usually, the error of our ways is not revealed to us until we lose a job. Then we ask ourselves, "Who will provide for me now?" The truth is, God is the only one who can truly provide for us. God has given us talents and creativity. It is through those gifts from Him that we can obtain all we need, and far more.

God wants us to be successful so we can share with others. We should not attain our goals and then just walk away. God wants us to share our knowledge, to teach others and guide them so they can make their dreams come true, too. God also wants us to share our prosperity with those less fortunate. We should never forget those who need our help. As Jesus says in Matthew 26:11, "For you always have the poor with you. . ."

God wants you to be prosperous. Never forget that He is the source of your welfare, and He wants you to share your blessings with others.

This book of the law shall not depart out of your mouth; you shall meditate on it day and night. . . For then you shall make your way prosperous, and then you shall be successful.

Joshua 1:8

||||||||||||||||||||||||||||||||||||||||||||||||||||||||||||||||||||||||||||||||||||||||

"What we are is God's gift to us. What we become is our gift to God."

—Eleanor Powell

||||||||||||||||||||||||||||||||||||||||||||||||||||||||||||||||||||||||||||||||||||||||

50

God IS Your Choice

Every moment of every day, we are making ourselves into who we should be. God's way should be our choice.

WE OFTEN FEEL OVERWHELMED by expectations of who we *should* be. Almost everywhere we look, there are advertisements portraying what we should look like, what we should purchase, what we should wear, how we should wear it—and the list goes on and on.

In today's world we are told that we should always be buying more, making our lives feel like a constant process of addition and subtraction. Also, all these different possibilities can overwhelm us. They can blind us like a snowstorm. Many struggle with maintaining good relationships under the constant pressure of social expectations. For some, the stress can manifest itself in physical problems such as panic attacks, difficulty concentrating, depression, or anxiety.

It can become increasingly difficult to focus on what will really bring satisfaction in our lives. We face the evils of this world each day; it's hard to ward off harshness and negativity. But this is no excuse for hurting others in thought or deed.

We must remember that, above all else, God's way should be our choice. God must be the foundation of every thought and deed in our lives. It is He who gives us the strength to go on. As the Bible says in 2 Timothy 1:6–7:

> *For this reason I remind you to rekindle the gift of God that is within you through the laying on of my hands; for God did not give us a spirit of cowardice, but rather a spirit of power and of love and of self-discipline.*

Every moment of every day, we are making ourselves into who we should be. With our thoughts, intentions, and actions, we have the ability to act as God wants us to.

God loves His creation, and He will never desert us. Use God as your guide, and be sure to welcome your fellow man into your heart.

Indeed, the word of God is living and active, sharper than any two-edged sword, piercing until it divides soul from spirit, joints from marrow; it is able to judge the thoughts and intentions of the heart.

Hebrews 4:12

51

God IS Fair

Before we pass judgment on others, let's be reminded
of how much mercy has been extended to us.
Remember, each one of us deserves an opportunity
to make changes in our lives.

A T ONE TIME OR ANOTHER, each one of us has been
guilty of passing judgment on somebody else.

We may judge those close to us or someone we hardly
know. We may even look down on someone who doesn't have
certain possessions. When we see people who are lacking, it
can be easy to assume the worst about their character; we
may think that they don't have what we have because they are
lazy, unintelligent, or unable.

The Bible warns us about judging others in Matthew 7:1–5:

Do not judge, so that you may not be judged. For with the judgement you make you will be judged, and the measure you give will be the measure you get. Why do you see the speck in your neighbour's eye, but do not notice the log in your own eye? Or how can you say to your neighbour, "Let me take the speck out of your eye," while the log is in your own eye? You hypocrite, first take the log out of your own eye, and then you will see clearly to take the speck out of your neighbour's eye.

God does not want us to judge others. Instead, we should render mercy and compassion to one another.

Our God is a merciful and fair God. Let us not forget how many times God has had mercy on us when we deserved worse, yet God allowed us to come out of a situation unscathed. Before we pass judgment on others, let's be reminded of how much mercy has been extended to us.

Remember, each one of us deserves an opportunity to make changes in our lives, no matter what we may have done. As long as we have breath in our bodies, there is always hope for all.

God is great. Let us always keep an open mind and refrain from judging others.

Your righteousness is like the mighty mountains, your judgements are like the great deep; you save humans and animals alike, O Lord.

Psalm 36:6

52

God IS Your Foundation

Let us be sure God is the foundation of our lives.
Creating a foundation that rests on God is the only
thing that will get us through the unseen pitfalls of
life, and it is the only thing that is certain.

ONE OF LIFE'S GREATEST OBSTACLES occurs when we neglect to build a solid foundation for ourselves. With all of life's uncertainties, groundwork that is not solid can shift easily. No matter how much time we spend establishing a concrete map or direction for our own lives, and no matter how much we hope that it will all pan out the way we direct it, life's unseen pitfalls and its ups and downs always come along. Creating a foundation that rests on God is the only certainty.

I am reminded of a story of a woman I knew. Although she was married and had been blessed with several children and a good job, her life was in turmoil. To those who knew her, it seemed there was nothing she couldn't do. She was active in her community, attended school meetings, and served in her church. If there was a need to be met, she was there to assist. She never sought recognition or expected anything in return. Yet she felt overwhelmed by her life's responsibilities.

This young lady had a foundation (her family, friends, church, and community), but like concrete, the important ingredients needed to be properly mixed. She lacked the most important element needed to stabilize the foundation: God. After carefully revaluating where she was, this young woman repositioned herself. *She changed her way of thinking and sought God first.*

A foundation must effectively support the next layer of material that will be placed on top of it. God is stable and consistent. He will never be swayed or moved; He will never waver in His concern for us. He is our rock, our foundation. God is the only foundation that can support us as the weight of more and more challenges are added to our lives.

God is always present in our lives. He has a purpose for each one of us. If we take hold of God's hand and allow Him to lead us through life's twists and turns, the effects of the inconsistencies in our lives will be lessened. Confusion will decrease.

The next time you experience discomfort from the ebb and flow of life's inconsistencies or a feeling of turmoil, check out the map that you have planned. Is God the compass directing you? Is He the main ingredient in your foundation?

God is the most important part of the equation. Let us be sure He is the foundation of our lives.

But ask in faith, never doubting, for the one who doubts is like a wave of the sea, driven and tossed by the wind; for the doubter, being double-minded and unstable in every way, must not expect to receive anything from the Lord.

James 1:6–8

Closing Thoughts

GOD IS GREAT in so many ways.
     He is a true friend, a compassionate Father, and an example for us to follow. Above all, God is Love.

God's unconditional love extends beyond our imagination.

God is all you have read in this book. . . and more.

Even after you have finished reading *God is Great*, may you seek to learn more, everyday, about God and your relationship with Him. Take the time to give thanks for the many things He has made possible. Do not hesitate to rely on Him when times are hard.

No matter what lies ahead for you, may the book *God is Great* always remind you of the magnificent role God plays in your life.

God is great for each one of us, every day of our lives.

About the Author

PASTOR TONIA JENKINS is a preacher, teacher, wife, and mother of three children. She was born in New York and raised in the Bronx. Tonia graduated from Adalai Stevenson High School and later attended The Metropolitan College of New York and the New York School of The Bible at Calvary Baptist Church. Tonia and her husband, Pastor Darren Jenkins, are currently pastoring the New Hope Love Center Ministry Church, which provides help and hope for those in need. Tonia has chosen to dedicate her life to helping others so that they can focus on God's unique plan of destiny for their lives.